UNBROKEN BREAD

MIKE ROOT

UNBROKEN BREAD

HEALING

WORSHIP

WOUNDS

COLLEGE PRESS PUBLISHING COMPANY • JOPLIN, MISSOURI

Library of Congress Cataloging-in-Publication Data

Root, Mike
    Unbroken bread: healing worship wounds / Mike Root.
      p.   cm.
    Includes bibliographical references.
    ISBN 0-89900-779-1 (pbk.)
    1. Public worship.   2. Church controversies.   I. Title.
BV15.R665 1997
264–dc21   97-11028
                                                         CIP

ACKNOWLEDGMENT

When the last word of a book has been written, you tend to stand up and cheer, "Look what I've done!" Every author is entitled to a few moments of prideful exhilaration before reality sets in. This book would not be possible if it were not for a "bunch of good folks" who helped. There is a lifetime of teachers, preachers, brethren, and other authors who all have their hand in some part of this book. One hand placed a plethora of red marks all over the manuscript (and *Life's Cobwebs*) and helped make the final book presentable. A tremendous debt is owed to Julie Fry's good eyes, red pen, and ability to read a manuscript with three small children hanging on her. Another good friend and mentor who wielded a mean red pen was Dr. Mac Jacobs, a Professor and minister in Calgary, Canada. Thanks for your help and sacrifice, Brother Mac. Also I must offer a special word of appreciation to the wonderful brethren at College Press. John Hunter and the rest of the folks in Joplin are simply wonderful. In the three books that they have published for me, they have been gracious, encouraging, and totally Christian about everything. Thank you, College Press, and may God continue to bless you. And Steve, I haven't forgotten the Three Stooges tie I promised!

DEDICATION

This book is humbly dedicated to all the beautiful brethren at Altamesa who have loved me and my family for the last seven years. Thanks for being my church family. Thanks for sticking with me through the good times and the bad. Thanks for believing in me. Most of all, thanks for helping me to look forward to heaven because I know you will be there. A big thank you to my fellow partners in the Gospel, Cary, Patty, Scott, Georgia, Joanie, and Judy, who make "going to work" a daily blessing. You're great and I love you.

TABLE OF CONTENTS

INTRODUCTION

God didn't like Cain's offering, but He loved Abel's. Did you ever wonder how Abel knew what God wanted? Obviously, there had been some unrecorded communication to them from God or the rebuke of Cain would have been unjustified. The Genesis account tells us that God "had no regard" for the offering of Cain (4:5). I had always assumed that the problem was Cain's offering of fruit of the ground while Abel offered the firstlings of his flock. It is simply a case of Cain offering the wrong thing and thus offering unacceptable worship to God.

When you look closer at the story you see a deeper problem. When God confronted Cain, His concern was for his attitude. He asked, "Why are you angry? And why has your countenance fallen?"(v. 6). Could it be that God had no regard for Cain's offering because his heart was not as it should have been? Could the admonition from God for him to "do well" really be referring to a weakening faith that

Satan was "crouching at the door" to exploit? Could it be that the first serious conflict between men, between brothers, was a conflict over worship; and even then and for evermore, what God wanted was a loving heart?

I think it is safe to say that the number one area of strife in the Brotherhood today is over worship and worship styles. A small part of the strife involves doctrinal differences, but the vast majority of the problems stems from opposing preferences.

It is the intent of this book to examine worship and the assembly in the light of what Scripture really says, and to help heal some of the dissension that seems to be growing each day. This is not a tradition-bashing book, but you will be challenged to test our traditions against the Truth. The important thing is not to change our traditions, but to recognize them as traditions and not doctrine.

In *Spilt Grape Juice* I introduced the thesis that New Testament worship was not a place, time, or event, but our life. The Christian assembly was never called or intended to be our worship. It is simply a togetherness tool to encourage, equip, and edify one another, to help us be living sacrifices before God. *Unbroken Bread* is not a *Spilt Grape Juice, Part Two*, but it is a deeper study of that thesis, with special emphasis given to what the assembly should be, why it is a source of strife, and how we should respond to this problem as Christians. It is my prayer that you will open your mind, your heart, and your Bible as you read this. Like *Spilt Grape Juice*, this is not a scholarly theological work, but rather a devotional study for all of us average folks who just want to understand this subject.

I offer one last suggestion before you jump into chapter 1. As you read this book and you find yourself getting, like Martha, "worried and bothered about so many things," keep reading. The last few chapters may surprise you.

SECTION ONE
Restored Worship

CHAPTER 1
Unbroken Bread

Usually we just went out for hamburgers, but for some reason this Sunday night we ended up at one of those over-priced vogue restaurants that advertises "No rules, just right." Going out to eat after the Sunday evening worship services is just one of our traditions (Yes, I actually believe in traditions — especially the ones involving prime rib!). Since it was a popular restaurant and always crowded, the only place they could squeeze our crew of twenty in happened to be next to the bar section. So there we were, twenty Christians packed around three tables designed to hold four each, sitting next to a large gathering of folks who hadn't heard Paul's admonition to "not get drunk with wine, for that is dissipation, but be filled with the Spirit" (Eph 5:18). I don't know if they were "drunk with wine" but I do know that we were "filled with the Spirit." I know it sounds scary, but the Bible says it, and I believe it.

Guess which group was the rowdiest? That's right, the

fresh-from-the-assembly-of-saints-group, who were thoroughly loving one another's presence. We drew plenty of stares and several comments about "what's really in that ice tea," but I could also see some wondering eyes that were saying, "Boy I'd like to be part of that group, because they're having so much fun." WE WERE! We'd had a great Sunday filled with enriching togetherness in the name of Jesus and to the glory of God. We were excited about the Vacation Bible School we'd just finished the Wednesday before where we averaged over a thousand children and adults attending each night. We were thrilled by the challenge of a new building program. Most of all, we were excited about the future of God's church and the positive changes that were taking place. We couldn't contain ourselves! There was a lot to talk about, share, dream, and give thanks for. We were glad to be children of God and to be together.

When the waitress brought out their famous hot bread on a wood cutting board, a brother sitting at the middle of the table got the job of cutting slices for everyone else. The problem was that he couldn't cut and serve fast enough for the size group we had, and it didn't help that we were all giving him a hard time about being slow. Finally, in exasperation, he held up the small loaf of bread and said, "Let's just do this like they did it in the Bible," and he broke off a chunk for himself and passed the bread to the next person, who also broke off a piece. Thus the bread was passed, broken, and shared. In the midst of the fun and food, I was struck by the profound symbolism of that simple act — an act that in our modern culture seemed silly and even a little unsanitary. Still, it spoke powerfully to me that as Christians, we had a common love and a common Lord just like the saints of the New Testament, and just like them, we broke bread together.

As I write this I have been a Christian for over thirty years, and as I have expanded my mind by growing "in the nurture and admonition of the Lord," I have also expanded my waist by the nourishments shared with brethren through the years. In fact, I see myself as something of an expert in breaking bread with brethren. Little did I know that my three decades of research into Christian culinary practices would lead to such weighty conclusions. We've all enjoyed potlucks, cookouts, banquets, dinner clubs, dinner-on-the-grounds, fellowship dinners, ministry dinners, staff lunches, new member dinners, small group dinners, Sunday dinners, and a hundred other occasions when brethren break bread together, and that doesn't count all the doughnuts we've broken together too. I hope we never stop doing it and also hope we never start counting the calories involved. My research has taught me many things, not the least of which is a need for an inexhaustible supply of Tums™, but here is one indisputable fact: GREAT THINGS HAPPEN WHEN GOD'S PEOPLE BREAK BREAD TOGETHER.

IT'S A BIBLE THING!

Throughout history bread has always been one of the staples of life. While it's still true today, the word "bread" is just as likely to be referring to lucre as to loaves, but even that connotation comes from the power derived as a result of possessing bread. In Bible times, however, obtaining bread was a matter of survival, especially for the vast majority of people who happened to also be poor. Breaking bread together was a significant act of sharing. For the people of God, bread represented God's love. Through the giving of bread, be it seed, grain, loaf, or manna, God provided for His people and they thankfully remembered His goodness every time they partook of it. As a result of this, they had a high respect and reverence for bread. It was "because of this reverence for bread, one never cut bread with a knife. One broke the bread with respect, grateful for God's gift of the bounty of the land."[1]

It was because of this connection with God through the symbol of bread that the breaking or sharing of bread became such a spiritual activity. While hospitality was and is a virtue in the Middle East, and while a spiritual significance is clearly part of many Old Testament accounts of breaking bread, it is in the New Testament that we truly see an eternal quality inseparably bound with this temporal act.

Jesus changed the significance of bread breaking when He declared Himself to be "the bread of life" (John 6:35). As bread takes care of our physical hunger, He alone can take care of our spiritual hunger, and we will never be hungry again. I wonder how often He held up a chunk of bread at a meal and used it as a powerful visual aid in teaching that lesson. Not only was bread a symbol for Jesus, the breaking of bread was an opportunity.

Several times through the years I've had a brother or sister in Christ, who must have been suffering from acute spiritualitis, say to me, "All we ever do when we get together is eat. Can't we get together and do something without food being part of it?" You can see their mind working it out; food is physical; fasting is spiritual; therefore, spiritual things don't involve food. Other than being illogical and unbiblical, it sounds like we should attend Weight Watchers on Sunday instead of meeting with the rest of the church. I have often responded to those individuals by asking them if they ever noticed how much of Jesus' personal teaching was done at a meal? It is really astonishing to discover how many eternal truths were shared during the breaking of bread. As Robert Morgan points out in his book *Who's Coming to Dinner? Jesus Made Known in the Breaking of Bread*,

> Jesus' method of teaching was to use every opportunity at his disposal to communicate his message. He focused on the obvious to make his point to those who followed him.

> Mealtime provided Jesus with the platform to make
> known his teachings on matters such as forgiveness, salva-
> tion, humility, servanthood, justice, and life.[2]

This practice didn't stop with His death. Jesus appeared
several times after His resurrection to break bread with His
disciples and encourage them to get ready for what was to
come. In Luke 24:13-35, He walked with the men on the
road to Emmaus and ended His time with them by sharing
a meal. It was only after "He took bread, blessed and broke
it" that they recognized Him. Later they would recount
how "He was recognized by them in the breaking of the
bread." (v. 35) It seems that breaking bread was clearly an
identifying characteristic that might have appeared on a
Roman "Wanted" poster.

Later, when He appeared in the room with His apostles,
and still later when He fixed breakfast for them on the
beach, the breaking of bread was central to their relationship. (See Luke 24:36-48; John 21:1-14.)

Since they broke bread at nearly every post-resurrection
appearance of Jesus, it should not be surprising that just a
few days later, when the church began, breaking bread
together was an ongoing and integral part of what
Christians did. In fact, it could be said that the purpose for
Christians coming together at any time was to break bread,
either figuratively or literally.

KNEADFUL WORSHIP

After centuries of having assembled in a tabernacle or
the temple, what did God use to give the first 3000 babes
in Christ a sense of identity, a sense of belonging, a sense
of continuity, but still keep a sense of a changed covenant?
They had been waiting for the Messiah to come, and He
did, and they had been told what to do to be joined with
Him, and they did. Now what? What did they need most?

How were they going to grow spiritually and maintain unity in the midst of a belligerent society? There was no one to copy because there had never been a New Testament church before! This was ground zero for the biggest spiritual explosion that ever hit the world — and what did they do?

This would have been the perfect time to point out the importance of going to church on Sunday morning, Sunday night, and mid-week. What a great time to make clear which hours and places were the most holy and spiritual. This was the absolute best time to explain the difference between formal and informal worship and how to keep the balance between horizonal and vertical worship. What an opportune place to clarify the tremendous difference an "opening" or a "closing" prayer makes in terms of acceptable worship to God.

Maybe the Holy Spirit whispered to Peter and the others a message similar to the one in the old preacher's joke. Remember the note he got from his wife that said KISS and he later found out that rather than being a term of endearment it meant "Keep It Short Stupid"? Peter must have been told to "Keep It Simple Simon," because the major thrust of their directions for the new converts seems to have been "Stick together and help each other." So, WHAT DID THEY DO? Those first Christians became a bread breaking, fellowshiping, sharing, united, praying, studying, and growing bunch of fools — for Christ's sake!

Slowly read this well-known passage from Acts 2 and pay close attention to the language of togetherness. Three thousand "received his word and were baptized" on the day of Pentecost. Here's what they did next:

> And they were **continually devoting themselves** to the apostles' teaching and to **fellowship**, to the **breaking of bread** and to **prayer**. And **everyone kept feeling a sense of awe**; and many wonders and signs were taking place through the apostles. And **all those who had**

believed were together, and had all things in common; and **they** began selling **their property and possessions**, and were **sharing them with all, as anyone might have need**. And **day by day** continuing with **one mind in the temple**, and **breaking bread from house to house, they were taking their meals together with gladness and sincerity of heart, praising God**, and **having favor with all the people**. And the Lord was **adding to their number** day by day those who were being saved (vv. 42-47).

Every time I read that passage I am struck by the simplicity of New Testament Christianity. Look at the highlighted words again. Isn't it simply saying that Christians are people who love God and each other? Don't we see in these verses the very essence of what God wanted from the very beginning, which was "Love God with all your heart . . . . and your neighbor as yourself"? Isn't this passage describing people whose lives are saturated with sharing? There is a spirit of togetherness in these verses that speaks to the heart of what being a child of God is all about. We see them breaking the bread of devotion, the bread of prayer, the bread of excitement in Jesus, the bread of compassion, the bread of sacrifice, the bread of unity, the bread of hospitality, the bread of thanksgiving, the bread of joyful hearts, and the bread of numerical growth, just to name a few. This is why God wants His people to get together! IN ALL THE INSPIRED WRITINGS OF THE NEW TESTAMENT, THE ONLY REASON WHY GOD WANTS CHRISTIANS TO ASSEMBLE TOGETHER IS TO BREAK BREAD. HE WANTS US TO DO IT TODAY JUST LIKE THEY DID IN THE NEW TESTAMENT — NO MORE AND CERTAINLY NO LESS!

Whether it's the temple porch, a living room, a hillside, a prison, or a building specially constructed for Christians, God's people meet only to reap the benefits of togetherness. These benefits can't be obtained alone, even though

God is as much in attendance with the lone sentry as He is with the encampment of His army. And while we can dine alone on "The Bread of Life," it's only when we are together with Family that it becomes a banquet, a celebration of beggars who "hunger and thirst after righteousness."

You can sing when you're all by yourself, and you should. God hears the heart singing in the shower as well as the congregation singing the Hallelujah Chorus. You can pray and study by yourself, and you'd better — if you want to have a deeper relationship with God and Jesus. But James wrote that the "effective prayer of **a** righteous **man** can accomplish much" (Jas 5:16). There's power in prayer whether its one or one thousand doing the praying. The same is true of studying. "Let the word of Christ richly dwell within you," declared Paul, and that's on-top-of or in-spite-of what everyone else may do (Col 3:16).

Giving is probably one of the most personal and private things that we do. Each one of us must give as each of us has "purposed in **his** heart; not grudgingly or under compulsion; for God loves **a cheerful giver**" (2 Cor 9:7). The collection is simply an expedient way to gather it all up. In fact, the spirit of cheerful giving is a way of life and not just a check dropped in a tray on Sunday morning. Again, you could mail it and not be violating any New Testament principle about giving.

Why one could even break off a piece of unleavened bread, offer thanks, eat it, and meditate on Jesus' sacrifice, one's own spiritual condition, and look forward to His return, and do it all alone. Then do it again with the fruit of the vine — all alone. That's what many do on Sunday morning — they just happen to be surrounded by a building full of people. Is it any less a memorial feast that honors Jesus if one takes it alone?

What's the point? Singing, praying, studying, giving, and reflecting on Jesus are all tremendous tools for spiritual growth that can and should be done when you are alone, but what you can't do all by yourself is BE TOGETHER and reap the benefits of breaking bread together. The New Testament Christians assembled to break bread, not because they needed to sing, pray, study, give, and meditate on Jesus. These activities, and many others, were all tools to enhance their togetherness, and not rites or rituals to be performed.

DISCUSSION QUESTIONS

1. What are some of your most memorable fellowships? What made them so special?

2. What does "breaking bread" bring to mind for you?

3. What are some natural lessons that come from thinking of Jesus as "the Bread of Life?"

4. Why do we tend to think of breaking bread or sharing a meal as a non-spiritual activity?

5. Compare Acts 2:41-47 to what your church does. What is different? Why is it different?

6. How would you describe the sense of "togetherness" that you feel in your assembly?

CHAPTER 2
Loaf Looking

    While there are several allusions to Christian assemblies in the New Testament, there is not one single description of an assembly that records everything they did. In fact, in the grand scheme of things written in the Bible, there is comparatively very little written about the Christian assembly. It is really amazing that we know so much about it and are so sure about how it is supposed to be, when it's almost an afterthought in the Scriptures. When compared to the amount of attention given in the New Testament to the life and teachings of Jesus, mission work and evangelism, unity and Christian character, and the supremacy of love, the Christian assembly is nearly a footnote. Yet for some reason it is the focal point of our religion. Have we gone from simple bread breaking, a time to build one another up spiritually, to building a cathedral to religion made from all the dried out loaves of bread that throughout the centuries have gone unbroken?

The most often referred to passages of Scripture when we study the assembly are Acts 2, Acts 20, and 1 Corinthians 11–14. Acts 2:42-47, which we've already looked at, is describing the lifestyle faith of the first Christians. It included daily bread breaking, and the sharing of spiritual and physical blessings on all levels, at all times. In 1 Corinthians 11–14 Paul is attempting to correct some serious problems that the Corinthians were having in their assembly times. Their problems centered around misusing spiritual gifts, being inconsiderate of one another's needs, and forgetting the whole purpose of the assembly, which was "Let all things be done for edification" (1 Cor 14:26). Actually, a large part of their problem centered around a misunderstanding of and the abuse of breaking bread.

Acts 20 provides us with an excellent example of how simple the New Testament assembly was, and how the breaking of bread was central to both the simplicity and the togetherness. Paul and his missionary team spent a week in Troas. As Luke records it, "And on the first day of the week, when we were gathered together to break bread, Paul began talking to them . . . and he prolonged his message until midnight." Luke then tells the story of Paul healing Eutychus, who had fallen from the third floor window after being overcome by sleep. He then described how the rest of the assembly time went, "And when he had gone back up, and had broken the bread and eaten, he talked with them a long while, until daybreak, and so departed" (Acts 20:7-11).

Sounds just like last Sunday's worship assembly at your church, doesn't it? As my kids would say, "NOT!" It sounds to me like there was more "eatin' and preachin'" done in that assembly than most of us see in a year of church-going! Take out the story of Eutychus, which I'm sure Paul wished the Holy Spirit had done, and you have a wonderfully uncomplicated illustration of what the Christian assembly was meant to be — simple bread breaking among folks who love God and each other.

If we can get beyond using Acts 20:7 as a proof-text for having the Lord's Supper every first day of the week, we will see, and not see, several things that should raise an eyebrow or two. Here are some questions that come to my unorthodox mind:

1. Did this assembly begin at the appropriate time on Sunday morning?

2. Since Paul preached until midnight, was that midnight Sunday, according to the modern time, which starts at 12:01 A.M., or was it according to Jewish time when the Sunday began at 6:01 P.M. our Saturday, and would thus make this midnight our Saturday night?

3. Was this a formal worship or an informal devotional?

4. Where are the prayers? Especially the opening and closing prayers?

5. How did they know when the worship stopped and the fellowship started? (Especially with no closing prayer to make it clear)

6. Where's the singing?

7. Did they have a schedule of events, a program of services, or a sundial on the pulpit? Did they have a pulpit?

8. Did they serve the bread and wine from the front or rear of the room?

9. Did only men do the serving of communion? Did they have those pretty round cup holder trays with a cross on top?

10. It was the first day of the week and there was a visiting missionary — so why doesn't Luke mention an offering?

11. Assuming they did have prayers, did they "lift up holy hands?"

12. Which part of this was Bible class and which was worship?

13. Where's the invitation song?

14. Where's the "call to worship?"

15. Where's the praise team?

16. Since a minister can't be effective and look professional without a tie on, did Paul wear one? (Sorry, I had to ask!)

17. Did they understand that the many hours they spent in that warm, lit-by-oil-lamp room, was worship? Did they understand that they were "coming to worship" and later being "dismissed from worship?"

18. Did they believe that Christians had to meet in an "upper room?"

19. The first bread breaking in this passage was probably the Lord's Supper and the second breaking of bread was probably a meal. Did they see the first as completely spiritual and the second as completely social?

20. Was the meal "potluck" or catered?

While you are stewing over these questions, and maybe asking a few of your own, I'd like to describe what this Troas congregation did that night. Using the Bible, historical accounts, and a vivid imagination, here is what I see.

Sopater, Aristarchus, Secundus, Gaius, Timothy, Tychicus, and Trophimus had been with the Troas brethren for several days prior to Paul and Luke's arrival. The entire team had been meeting with Christians, encouraging and teaching them, and sharing the Gospel with anyone who would listen. They shared meals with Christians and interested non-Christians, and they taught in homes, in public, and in synagogues. The arrival of Paul and Luke merely added another team to the outreach efforts and house-to-house edifying that had been taking place.

The Sabbath day's rest ended about 6 P.M., and all the Christians made their way to a third floor room that was big enough to hold the entire group. After greetings, introductions, and the sharing of victories in Christ, they settled down to break bread together. It was their custom to partake of the Lord's Supper on the first day of the week, and as the sun set on the sabbath day it ushered in the new day, Sunday. "Paul began talking to them" about what the bread and wine represented. He explained to them that the spiritual supper was a time of premier togetherness. Together they were to reflect on what Jesus had done to save them, and together they were to examine their hearts and recommit to living for Him. Their togetherness was to also include a shared anticipation of the return of Jesus to gather His people to eternity.

These were not merely things they reflected on in the privacy of their individual minds. These were things they shared, discussed, and confessed to one another. It was a time of opening hearts, recommitting their love, and shedding tears of thanksgiving. The unleavened bread and the fruit of the vine provided a visual focus for their sharing, their remembering, and their growing. They may have been partaking of emblems, but it was primarily a partaking of love.

The word that is used in this passage for "spoke to" or "talking to" is the word for "reasoned" or "discussed with."[3] Paul's teaching was not a one-way discourse, but rather an open forum, with discussion and interaction. Since Paul was the walking Word of God, there were lots of questions, and he patiently responded to each and every one. They hung on every word, not even noticing how late it was getting.

The assembly was brought to an abrupt halt by the sickening sound of Eutychus hitting the cobblestoned street below. The seeming tragedy was soon turned to triumph as Paul embraced his body and brought him back from the dead. After the healing, they returned to the upper room to break the bread of a shared meal and continue the discussion. Before they knew it, the sun was coming up and it was time for Paul to catch his ship and depart. For everyone else, it was the beginning of another normal day of work.

It's at this point that the "formula theologians" want to point out, "Since there are other places in the New Testament that describe prayer, singing, and contributions being part of the assembly, we must assume that the Troas church did these things in their assembly." That sounds reasonable, and it may be (not must be) the truth, but I suspect it comes more from a need to justify OUR traditional approach to the Christian assembly than from a need to be scripturally accurate. We meet to perform "the Five Acts of Worship" while the Troas brethren met to be together. Instead of having "acts" to perform, they had tools to use to enhance their edification in Christ. Just maybe, they chose to use only three of the many available to them because that was all they needed for their brief nine-to-twelve hour assembly.

With no patterns to follow, no schedules to keep, and no check lists to mark off, they spent their time together breaking bread. One of the things we MUST learn from this passage is that folks who "hunger and thirst after righteousness" will devour and share a lot of bread. They broke bread three ways.

First, they broke the bread of the Lord's Supper. The bread and wine were meant to generate reflection, discussion, confession, anticipation, bonding, and love, just to name a few. It was (and is) the ultimate fellowship meal that used the physical to trigger the deeply spiritual. This simple utilitarian meal was never meant to be buried by the gravy of mystery and magic, or seasoned with the spice of tradition and novelty. Communion means fellowship. The whole purpose of THE Communion was to enhance togetherness in Christ.

The second way they broke bread was by breaking the Bread of Life. Don't you wonder how much of Paul's teaching and discussion leading was about Jesus? Surely He was the main subject. After all, he made it clear that he ". . . did not come with superiority of speech or of wisdom . . . . For I determined to know nothing among you except Jesus Christ, and Him crucified" (1 Cor 2:1-2). This was the way he did all his mission work. Everything they shared that long evening and morning would have centered on Christ. It would have been either the life of Christ, living in Christ, or living eternally with Christ. For Paul, there was no other subject.

The third way they broke bread was, oddly enough, by breaking bread. They shared a meal together. This is what the church in Jerusalem did, according to Acts 2, and even though they abused it, it was what the church in Corinth did too. (See 1 Cor 11:16-34.) This literal breaking of bread was as much a part of their togetherness and edification as the first two. All three of these bread breaking activities were important elements in helping the church to "preserve the unity of the Spirit in the bond of peace" (Eph 4:3). When that happens, God is truly worshipped.

THE BREADFAST OF CHAMPIONS

Is it possible for a family of Christians to assemble and not participate in any of these three kinds of bread breaking? I wish the answer to that was "It's impossible," but unfortunately I think it happens regularly. When Christians meet together and perform rituals, with each person staying in their own little private meditative shell, and there is no interaction, intimacy, and no sharing, then THERE IS

31

NO BREAKING OF BREAD. We can call it worship, church, services, a religious gathering, a bingo party, or whatever we want, but it really is a memorial to UNBROKEN BREAD and a mockery of New Testament Christianity.

When was the last time you thought of the Lord's Supper as breaking bread together? In most assemblies it's a marvel of modern efficiency. The expected and theologically correct words are said over the pre-perforated crackers and the plastic disposable shot-glasses, all of which are appropriately arranged in shiny gold or silver serving trays, and served by pallbearers in a precharted pattern to insure that everything is done "decently and in order." The Lord's table is not in our hearts, but rather it's that huge, gaudy altar down front that must not be removed or people feel like they're not "gathering around the table." We must not talk, sing, or in anyway interact, because even though it's the event the Bible calls "fellowship," we know it's first and foremost a private time of introspection. Somehow Jesus and togetherness got lost in the arguing about serving communion from the front or back, whether or not we can sing or read Scripture during the passing of the trays, and whether it's okay to have crosses on top of our tray covers.

IF THERE IS NO REAL SHARING, THERE IS NO REAL BREAKING OF BREAD.

I am always humbled when a brother prays before I preach that God will "be with Mike as he breaks unto us the Bread of Life." I am also challenged to consider the implication of that request. For one thing, to break the Bread of Life is to share Jesus. Am I sharing Jesus in my sermon? I've heard many supposed Bread breakers who preached half-hour or three-quarter-hour sermons and almost never mentioned Jesus. They talked about orthodoxy, social ills, and political concerns, but they really didn't break the Bread of Life. Sometimes preachers preach about what's wrong with everybody else and never mention what's right about Jesus — everything.

Another implication of breaking the Bread of Life is the breaking part. As I have attempted to point out, breaking is sharing, but it must be real sharing, not just assumed sharing. When you break bread with someone you both tear off a real piece of bread and you both really eat it together. It is participating. It is two-way involvement. There are two speakers and two listeners. While preaching is intended to be a sharing of a message, sometimes, because of our traditional thinking on formal public speaking, the sharing is only one-way. There's no interaction, no question and answer time, no feedback, and no reciprocal learning. A presentation or a performance is not the same as sharing/breaking. Someone says, "But that's what Bible class is for." Wonderful, but most folks believe that Bible class is not THE assembly and therefore not as important as "the formal worship." That's why twenty to thirty percent of our members don't attend Bible class. In essence we are confessing that sharing/breaking the Bread of Life does not take place in the Christian assembly, but rather takes place at a less important time. I wonder if the folks in Acts 20 knew they were having a Bible class as well as a formal assembly?

Blame it on expediency, tradition, or plain old preferences, but it's still the truth; when there is no sharing, there is really no breaking of bread or Bread. This is not to say that there is never a time for a formal discourse or presentation, like Paul did on Mars Hill in Acts chapter 17, but I am saying that when Christians get together there should be REAL BREAKING (i.e., two-way sharing) of the Bread of Life. Preachers don't just hope that the brethren have caught the few crumbs we tossed their way, we must make sure of it. We must SHARE the Bread, not just pose with it!

DISCUSSION QUESTIONS

1. In what ways did the church at Corinth miss the point about breaking bread? (1 Cor.10-14)

2. How is the Christian assembly in Acts 20:7-11 like yours? What is different? Why?

3. How did you answer the list of questions about Acts 20 in this chapter?

4. Do you think there was more interaction between folks in the assembly during the New Testament times than there is today? Why?

5. Do you think all three types of Bread Breaking should be part of every assembly? Why or why not? When?

6. Is it possible for Christians to assemble and not do any of the three kinds of Bread Breaking? Why? When?

CHAPTER 3
Dough Rich but Bread Poor

My mother was a single parent and I was a "latchkey kid" long before either of those became social categories. We had plenty to eat and I always thought of her as a great cook, but as I look back on those bygone years I realize our meals were pretty basic. Because she worked all day and had an hour-long commute each way, our dinners consisted of meat, potatoes, and a vegetable. Usually the entire meal went from freezer to the table in a relatively short period of time. They were great meals, from a loving mother, who worked hard and endured tremendous difficulties to provide for her family. So this isn't an "I-came-from-a-poor-starving-family" confession, but rather a bread-time story.

I grew up thinking of bread as wrapping for peanut butter and jelly. Other than sandwiches and toast, our bread consumption was nearly nonexistent. On Sunday afternoons, when we had our biggest meal of the week, we did have rolls, but they were either "Brown and Serve" store-bought rolls, or the canned ones that the Pillsbury Dough Boy giggles about. Homemade bread was never missed because I never knew it was an option.

Then I got married to a beautiful Arkansas girl whose farm family had fresh baked rolls or biscuits at every meal. In keeping with her family tradition and her desire to be a wonderful wife, my new mate and I broke freshly baked bread every day, which deepened our relationship and broadened my waistline. I loved it (and her of course). There's no better fragrance that can fill a house than the smell of bread baking. I shudder to think about how many tons of bread I ate in those first few years, not to mention the butter I baptized each piece in.

A couple of years and pants sizes later, having fresh bread with my meal was "no big deal" anymore. In fact, I remember a dinner when we completely forgot to even put the bread on the table. Donna had placed the rolls back into the turned off oven to keep them warm and we didn't even miss them. At the end of the meal, when we were already filled with all the other good gifts on our table, she said, "Oh my, I forgot to put the rolls on the table!" To which I groaned, "I'm way too full to eat one now." So the bread went unbroken.

This little trip down our culinary memory lane reminds me of two important reasons why bread is unbroken: ignorance and complacency. In the early years of my life bread was unbroken because I just didn't know how good it really could be. I never missed what I never had. Later, however, when it was available, constant, and even expected, I took it for granted and it lost its attractiveness, its desirability.

The reason why Christians assemble and somehow manage to never really break bread is found in one or both of these same attitudes. Sometimes folks just don't know what they are missing. They've never experienced genuine sharing or intimacy in the assembly. They get too busy performing the "five acts" then leave spiritually malnourished as they survive on the crumbs of love picked up in the aisle or the foyer. "People of The Book" just don't know what The Book really says about Christian togetherness. They've been told, not shown in The Book, that the assembly is a formal, reverential, unemotional encounter with God. It's payback — "the least we can do for God!" It's solemn, so you must "wear your best for God." It's meditative because "The Lord is in His holy temple. Let all the earth keep silent before Him" (Hab 2:20). You are there only to please God because it is THE WORSHIP. It doesn't seem to bother anyone that there is absolutely NOTHING in the New Testament that substantiates any of these things! Is it any wonder that the real bread is unbroken!

Even when we understand and know that the assembly is for breaking bread, that is, genuine sharing through the Lord's Supper, the Bread of Life, and fellowship, we still struggle with complacency. Corinth is an excellent example of this problem. They were gung ho on liberty in Christ, but complacent about unity, togetherness, and being Christlike.

Because of their selfishness and bickering, Paul said, ". . . I do not praise you, because you come together not for the better but for the worse" (1 Cor 11:17). So they had clearly missed the reason for their coming together. The entire series of praises or condemnations in 1 Corinthians 11 is based on the extent to which they measured up to the foundational point of "Be imitators of me, just as I also am of Christ" (11:1). The Bread of Life was the standard by which all their actions were judged. So the first area of complacency was in forgetting to be Christlike. In terms of their assembly time, the first problem Paul mentions involves their coming together but coming all apart.

Paul said, "In the first place, when you come together as a church, I hear that divisions exist among you; and in part,

I believe it" (v. 18). He points out that there is a time and place for factions, but not "when you come together as a church." Unity is the very essence of what breaking bread is all about. Can you imagine brethren coming together to share Jesus, His supper, and His bounty and still being factious? It happens when we become complacent about what these are for.

Jesus instituted His supper during a dinner. It seems that the early Christians followed that pattern. The order was never an issue, but ignoring the purpose of the bread breaking, whether it was the meal or the Lord's Supper, was a big issue with Paul. He told them, "Therefore when you meet together, it is not to eat the Lord's Supper, for in your eating each one takes his own supper first; and one is hungry and another is drunk" (vv. 20-21).

Throughout the centuries many used these verses to prove the clear distinction that must exist between the social and the spiritual. They argue that the two must never mix. So we traditionally have our "Worship time" and then a separate "fellowship time." I believe that this is a gross misinterpretation of the text. There is nothing in the New Testament that suggests they made any such distinction. In this passage Paul is not condemning the "mixing" but rather the complete ignoring of "togetherness." The sin is in the phrase "each ONE takes HIS OWN." What they were doing was displaying a blatant disregard for others. Again, they violated the very essence of what bread breaking was for Christians. That is why Paul's prose screams out "What! Do you not have houses in which to eat and drink? Or do you despise the church of God, and shame those who have nothing? What shall I say to you? Shall I praise you? In this I will not praise you" (v. 22).

Wow! Paul couldn't praise them because they were not being imitators of Christ. They were being selfish and letting their appetites dictate what they did. Their meal wasn't a sharing experience but rather a showing experi-

38

ence. They were bringing excessive amounts of food and drink and only sharing them with their little group, when they wanted to, regardless of whether everyone else was ready or even present. Thus they were despising "the church of God," because it wasn't a church/togetherness activity. And they were shaming those in the congregation who had little or nothing to share with others. This wasn't the way the breaking of bread was supposed to be, either for the meal or the Lord's Supper. So Paul reminds them about what the Lord's Supper was meant to be and as far as breaking the bread of a shared meal he said, ". . . when you come together to eat, wait for one another." If you can't, ". . . eat at home."(See 1 Cor 11:1-34.)

To return to my personal parable, when my wife and I forgot to put the bread on the table, not only did it go unbroken, but it wasn't even missed. While we missed something good, it wasn't the reason for our meal and the bread of love and togetherness was still broken. The Corinthians broke bread, even to excess, but the bread of Christian fellowship went unbroken. Any congregation today would be hard pressed to have any more spiritual activities going on than the Corinthian brethren did, but they were still missing the main ingredient — love. It's no accident that 1 Corinthians 13, the great love chapter, is smack in the middle of Paul's discussion of spiritual gifts and the assembly. The biggest reason why there is so much divisiveness about our assemblies today is because the bread of love has gone unbroken for too many years. While love is the greater gift, it is also the greater reason for coming together.

CHRISTIANS FOR LOAF

The Root house is getting quieter each year. As I write this, last month our second daughter joined her older sister at college. We now have two empty bedrooms and a dinner table with the leaf removed. My son, our youngest, while he misses his sisters, is loving having the bathroom, the TV, and the third car all to himself. It was really hard driving off and leaving them at college. While I was sad, I didn't shed any tears until I got the first tuition bill. Actually, my wife and I have such busy schedules, and we are so happy that they are happy, that we don't spend a lot of time mourning over their absence. That is, until we sit down to dinner.

The circle is pretty small when we hold hands and have our prayer. It only takes a minute to set the table for three, and it only takes a few seconds for my son to report on his day. It's wonderful to have some uninterrupted quality time with him, but I sure do miss that time of reconnecting with each of my children. I miss their excited stories, their plans, their problems, and most of all their laughter. Dinner has always been a time of reconnecting for us — a time of remembering how much we love each other, and a time to remember our commitments to each other. The breaking of bread helps cement our family together.

Memories and pictures of families may center around Christmas, vacations, birthdays, and trips, but the real bonding of a family takes place in the simple acts of day-to-day sharing. Likewise, when the family of God comes together, it is a time to reconnect, to bond, to rejoice in our togetherness and our salvation. When we break bread, whether it's Jesus, His supper, or a meal, we are doing two essential things.

First we are communing. Personally, I believe this is one of the most overlooked and forgotten parts of New Testament Christianity. Communion comes from the Greek word *koinonia*. It means "a having in common, partnership, fellowship, denotes the sharing which one has in anything, a participation, fellowship recognized and enjoyed; thus it is used of the common experience and interests of

Christian men."[4] The *Expository Dictionary* then follows this definition with a plethora of Scripture references from the New Testament to show the many different times it is used.

This will be said again later, but it needs to be said here to make a point. Not once, ever, is the word "worship" used in the New Testament in connection with Christians in the assembly, but *koinonia* is consistently used.[5] Not only is it odd that we stress that the assembly is worship, but we demote fellowship to a secondary — after the closing prayer — purely social and optional kind of status. How did this happen? It comes from an obstinate, and doggedly determined desire to maintain tradition. We sure didn't get it from the Bible.

Communing, which is the very heart of bread breaking, is sharing. While we don't want to beat this point to death by going over it again, the emphasis is not on private meditation, but on togetherness. We share Him! We share His death, burial, and resurrection! We share an anticipation for His return! We share grace, love, redemption, and eternal life. We share songs, prayers, thoughts, problems, blessings, food, dreams, work, play, money, and encouragement. All three kinds of bread breaking are communion. If bread goes unbroken, then there is no communion. If we really want to restore New Testament Christianity, then it must include restoring *koinonia* to our assemblies. It's time for the return to the "old paths" to be more than fighting to restore 1945 assembly styles. When we have to wait for the closing prayer to enjoy real one another communing, something has gone terribly wrong.

The second essential part of bread breaking is renewing our covenant. As Robert Morgan points out in his book *Who's Coming To Dinner? Jesus Made Known in the Breaking of Bread*, one of the most important functions of bread breaking was that "it was used as a covenant. There are a number of covenant ceremonies in the Bible, but the breaking of bread or the shared bread seems to be the most prominent."[6]

A covenant is basically the making and keeping of a promise. In the Bible a covenant with God is usually a promise from man to obey God and a promise from God to bless man in return. In Genesis 17, Abraham was told to seal his promise with God by instituting circumcision, and by following God's commands. As a result, God would bless him materially, give him a son, and through that son all the nations of the earth would be blessed. This covenant was renewed with Isaac and Jacob. If Israel would be the people of God, then He would be their God and take care of them. There are scores of covenants with patriarchs, kings, prophets, and the whole nation of Israel.

In Genesis 31, Jacob and Laban were reconciled to one another after a stormy separation and bitterness. To seal what was called the covenant of Mizpah, Laban built a pillar of rocks as a memorial of their joint promises, and closed the agreement with a meal (v. 54).

Jesus used bread to describe the new covenant relationship that He had with His followers. He first reminded them that it was God who gave Israel the manna in the wilderness, not Moses. God was the One they had a covenant relationship with. And now God was providing for them again with a new covenant. He said, ". . . it is My Father who gives you the true bread out of heaven. For the bread of God is that which comes down out of heaven, and gives life to the world." They didn't completely understand Him, but they knew they wanted this special bread. So Jesus spelled out the new covenant for them, "I am the bread of life; he who comes to Me shall not hunger, and he who believes in Me shall never thirst" (John 6:32-35).

This is a very clear and simple covenant. We must come to Him and believe, and He will take care of every spiritual need. The covenant was Bread, the seal of the covenant was bread, and bread became the memorial of the covenant. Just a short time later, Jesus was reflecting on the one who would betray Him and He said, "He who eats My bread has lifted up his heel against Me" (John 13:18). In other words, Judas was not only going to betray Him, but he would be breaking the covenant relationship they had.

This was a new covenant because the commands were new. He said the new commandment was "that you love one another, even as I have loved you, that you also love one another. By this all men will know that you are My disciples, if you have love for one another" (John 13:34-35). Notice the clearly defined two parts. We love — He loved. Also notice the condition "if you have love for one another." To not love one another is to break the covenant we have made with Jesus.

So — when and where do we love one another? In theological theory? Monday through Saturday when we may never see another Christian? How about when we are together? The Christian assembly?

Every time we break the Bread of Life, we must be reminded of our covenant with Him. He loved us — we must love one another. Every time we break the unleavened bread and drink the wine we must remember our covenant with Him. It includes looking back to the cross, looking in to our hearts, and looking ahead to His coming (as 1 Cor 11:23-29 points out), but it's *koinonia*, or sharing it together that must also be a part of the covenant. It is the perfect love-one-another experience that is just as much a part of the whole agreement as when we promised to "do this in remembrance of" Him. And finally, every time we break the bread of a shared meal or any kind of fellowship, we must renew our covenant with Him, our promise to love one another as He loved us, and remember that He has and always will keep His word. Will we keep ours?

It is precisely because we have taken the covenant element out of our assemblies that folks can slip into the back of the auditorium, do their five part Sunday morning religious drill, and slide right out the door having never experienced *koinonia* but still feel acceptable before God. After all, they attended worship, right?

Throughout the years I've heard many sermons and read many articles about why Christians must not "forsake the assembly." The list is endless and mostly unbiblical. The only biblical reasons why the assembly is essential are communing with one another and renewing our covenant with one another. When we do that, we also commune with and renew our covenant with our Lord and Savior Jesus Christ. You will find no other reason in the New Testament for Christians to assemble. All the tools of togetherness mentioned in the Word are there to remind and enhance our communion and our covenant, with one another and with God.

KISS KISS!

I have mentioned in the past that I follow three rules in my preaching, teaching, and writing. I like to be simple, logical, and, most important of all, biblical. So, if I lost you in the verbiage, let me summarize my points.

1. Thesis: New Testament Christians assembled to break bread.
2. There are three kinds of bread breaking in the New Testament.
   (1) Breaking the Bread of Life = sharing Jesus
   (2) Breaking the bread of the Lord's Supper = sharing Jesus' death, resurrection, return, indwelling, and our personal struggles. Fellowship/*koinonia*.
   (3) Breaking the bread of a shared meal = sharing our material possessions and building unity and love.
3. There are two essential reasons why we must break bread together.
   (1) Communion = *koinonia*, sharing, participating, togetherness, closeness in Christ.

(2) Covenant = remembering our commitment to Jesus and the corresponding commitment to love one another.

Each of these points could and should have volumes written about them. Go for it! This is just a general introduction to set the stage for looking at an array of items dealing with worship and the Christian assembly. I will close this section with this observation:

It is amazing what one will see in the New Testament when one goes to it without any preconceived ideas of what should be found there.

DISCUSSION QUESTIONS

1. Do you experience genuine sharing or intimacy in the assembly? Why or why not?

2. What do you think about the statement "We must wear our best clothes to church for God?"

3. Are worship and fellowship two distinct and separate Christian activities?

4. What is it that changes a meal into real bread breaking?

5. When do you have *koinonia* in your assembly?

6. How important is a sense of covenant to a church family?

SECTION TWO
Revealed Worship

CHAPTER 4
The Field of Battle

I don't know if someone planted this thought in my head or if I simply reached this conclusion on my own, but here's my Thought for The Day:

THE OLDER I GET, THE DUMBER I REALIZE I HAVE BEEN.

Profound? Hardly. All of us have experienced the illumination of time and discovered that what we thought we fully understood was really only the surface of something much deeper and far more complex. Twenty-four years ago, I thought I knew all I needed to get married. I didn't. Twenty years ago, I just knew I was prepared for children. I wasn't. A quarter of a century ago, I thought I fully grasped the role of the preacher, but what I thought was "being prepared" actually was blissful ignorance.

The list is endless. Finances, politics, human relations, mechanics, taxes, carpentry, writing, and a host of other subjects, have all, at one time or another, proven to be incomprehensible to this highly educated scribe. What I thought I knew was insufficient, so I learned and usually was humbled to find out that it still wasn't enough.

Recently I set out to paint the outside of our house. I knew how to paint. I'd painted rooms on numerous occasions. But painting the inside of a house is not like painting the outside. The outside has to be prepared. I thought I could just pop open a can of paint, dip the brush in it, and slap some paint on the house. I ended up spending more time scraping, caulking, and repairing wood trim than I did painting. I felt like a little kid in need of a mentor. "How do you caulk around brick? How do you scrape gutters? Does aluminum need a coat of primer too?"

If you had asked me before I started if I knew all about painting a house, I'd have said, "Sure, any dummy can do that." Well I'm a much smarter dummy now and looking forward to the day I can afford to pay someone to paint the house for me.

There is no area of my life where this principle is more true than in the spiritual realm. It is really incredible to think of all the things I thought I knew, but in retrospect I realize were surface religion, borrowed faith, and hand-me-down theology. Two decades ago I had no questions and all the answers. Today I have some answers and a lot of questions, but far more peace. Back then I knew some Scriptures and I thought I was strong, while today I know a great many Scriptures and think of myself as weak. I have to be weak, because it's only in my weakness that Jesus can use me.

There was a time when "contending for the faith" meant being contentious about the faith. I wasn't teaching Scripture and proving Jesus to be the Lord and Savior of mankind. I was correcting brethren. I rebuked them for being unscriptural, liberal, and wishy-washy in their theology. Looking back, while I was fighting brethren about preferences, opinions, styles, and interpretations, souls were dying without Christ.

At the time, I soothed my conscience with the assurance that I was "fighting the good fight of faith." The problem was that doctrinal correctness became more important than grace, love, and forgiveness. Not only are these the greatest doctrines, but what I thought was doctrinal correctness was oftentimes only man's traditions, and I fought tooth and nail to protect them.

Back to the point; what I thought I knew was shallow and what I didn't know could have filled volumes. God allowed me to rediscover His love and the power of His grace, and "Eureka!" I was placed here to share the Gospel, not shred Christians. I don't mean to say that I have arrived, but I do regret the wasted energy that was spent drawing lines, leaping to conclusions, and making mountains out of molehills. I want to leave the line drawing to God, limit the leaping to joy, and only be concerned with the hill that held the Old Rugged Cross. That's why it pains me deeply to see brethren fussing and fighting about the assembly.

As mentioned, in the past the battle lines were clear. Today, I don't even understand why we fight. We're not arguing Scripture, debating theology, or standing tall for the faith. We've even ignored and rejected our Restoration slogans. We don't speak where the Bible speaks but rather scream where the Bible is silent. If you don't think that is true, just ask yourself this question: When was the last time someone complained about anything in the assembly and they based their complaint on a rational interpretation of Scripture? In the last half-dozen years there has not been a Sunday that several brethren in our congregation haven't complained about something that took place. Only two times have I heard a Scripture used to bolster the complaint and both times the passages were grossly taken out of context.

Since all of us "with all humility and gentleness, with patience, showing forbearance to one another in love" are "being diligent to preserve the unity of the Spirit in the bond of peace," how is it possible that the Christian assembly is a battleground today? (Eph 4:2-3). Why is it that nearly every congregation is struggling with members who are unhappy about what is supposed to be an edifying experience? Why are churches torn by members who want changes and members who resist change? Why are so many Christians miserable because their spiritual past or their spiritual future is threatened? How did the assembly ever get to be so important that our faith depends on getting what WE want that one hour on Sunday morning?

The questions are endless and so are the answers. Nevertheless, I want to suggest a few of the reasons why the assembly is a battleground today.

1. **Rituals, Ruts, and Routines**. When I was a youngster, I never-ever asked, "I wonder what's going to happen at church next Sunday morning?" I knew exactly what was going to happen. The same thing that happened every Sunday, the same way, the same schedule, the same format, and with the same results. Was that bad? Not necessarily. There is a great deal of comfort and security in predictability. Unfortunately, somewhere along the way, most of the folks at church forgot that the routine was a matter of choice and it became law. Predictability became the golden calf and woe be unto any young whippersnapper who suggested a change.

For many of those folks, such predictability was wonderful and I am sure their hearts were pure before God. For many of us though, the assembly became boring, the activities became meaningless rituals, and the intolerance became a threat. It would be easy to say at this point that it was a personal problem, but the truth is that it was a generational problem that soon worked its way into a sociological and theological problem, which made it a problem for all ages.

The church growth experts have written extensively on

this subject. Dr. John Ellas, in his book *Clear Choices For Churches*, described this as, not the Generation Gap, but rather "the Generation Gulf" because the differences between the two groups where so dramatic. The Gulf is between the Pre-World War 2 generation and the Post-World War 2 generation. He says, "Division between the pre- and the post-war generation is now considered so great that it is cross-cultural in nature. . . . Failure by church leadership to address generation gulf issues is a major source of increased church conflict." Dr. Ellas went on to point out that this conflict has "a repetitive ring" with one of the dominant issues being "worship activities (will it have contemporary elements or be all traditional?)"[7]

While I agree completely with that assessment and I would encourage you to read what Dr. Ellas and other experts say, I believe the results of church routines and rituals transcended generational lines. Many educated and open-minded Christians of all ages have rebelled against the religious ruts that have promoted legalism, driven young people away, and turned the assembly into a cold, lifeless charade of what we read about in the New Testament. There are plenty of pre-war men and women who know their Bibles and know there is room for freedom, flexibility, relevance, and tolerance. It is actually their loyalty to the Word and their desire to be Christlike that gives them the permission they need to reject religious ruts and insist on saving the next generation.

As wonderful as traditions are and as comfortable as routines make us, the insistence that a pre-war format be immutable, in spite of no biblical precedence, set the stage for later generations to challenge the status quo.

2. **The Rational Rule**. Throughout all religious history, few things have made more sense than the call to go back to the Bible and "be simply and only New Testament Christians." Alexander Campbell, Barton W. Stone, and the other Restoration leaders struck a receptive chord in the

hearts of thousands of people with that simple plea. In their day, and ours, people were disenchanted with the many denominations with their creeds and traditions. They welcomed the rational approach to studying the Scriptures. It made sense. If they did something in the New Testament — we must do it. If they didn't do something — we don't do it either. It was logical, uncluttered, simple, and safe. Most important of all, it was accurate and defendable. The Restoration churches became the supreme rational religion in the country. Others called us "narrow-minded literalists" and "fundamentalists," but that was just the price you paid when you stood for the truth.

If one argues against being rational does that make one irrational? Well, don't wait for me to argue against it. I believe with all of my heart that the Restoration plea is not only logical, but timeless. I am proud of a heritage that seeks biblical accuracy and spurns man-made creeds, manuals, and traditions. I thank God daily for allowing me to cross paths with New Testament Christians who helped me cut through the religious sludge and find the pure Word of God which is the only message that can save souls. I believe in the rational approach to interpreting the Scriptures. God's Word, even with its symbolism, occasional figurative language, and challenging paradoxes, is not irrational. It's the most logical book ever written. Jesus said, "What shall it profit a man if he gains the whole world but loses his own soul?" Who can argue with that?

So how does being a rational religion contribute to the assembly being a battleground? Like most good things, you can have too much of it. There are several ways that rational thinking can be theologically abused, but the two primary problems are formula theology and the exclusion of the Spirit.

Have I mentioned that I am not a mathematician? Anything that goes even a little bit beyond addition, subtraction, multiplication, and division quickly loses me.

Even with those basic math problems, I rarely follow the rules. When I add, subtract, multiply, or divide in my head, I move numbers around, round numbers off, add to subtract, subtract to add, and do things that are impossible to explain, but I usually get the right answer. It's fun and I achieve the correct end result. The process is not always as important as the finished objective.

In theology, I don't believe that the end justifies the means, but I also don't believe that spirituality can be reduced to a formula. Rational religion loves formulas. In an effort to be simple and logical, it can create religious equations that become mere creeds that are camouflaged by biblical language. For example:

What New Testament things do we emulate? Anything that is
    1. a command
    2. an example
    3. an implied inference

What must we do to become New Testament Christians?
    1. hear the word
    2. believe
    3. repent
    4. confess
    5. be baptized

What must we do to copy New Testament worship?
    1. pray
    2. sing
    3. give
    4. partake of the Lord's Supper
    5. study God's Word – preach

Are these wrong because they have been turned into a formula? Certainly not! The problem with a formula is that it becomes a "checklist" rather than a heart-level experience. The danger is that one may obey a process, a correct formula, and not obey the Lord who died to save him. I saw this happen on many occasions in the past when people were converted to "the plan of salvation" and then years later felt the need to be "baptized" into a relationship with Jesus. They had been taught the correct formula but not the correct faith.

It's this commitment to formula religion that helps drive the attitude that the assembly must not be altered. Brethren have had the formula, with appropriate accompanying Scriptures, drilled into their heads so thoroughly that accomplishing the "five acts" is the goal, whether or not edification ever happens.

The real irony is that worship is the one area where our rational movement leaps head first into the murky waters of irrational logic and calls it being heroic. It matters not that "the five acts of worship" is never found in Scripture, or that there are a dozen other things that the New Testament Christians did when they got together as well as those five. No one seems to notice that we don't have one single example of a New Testament assembly where all five of these acts were done. What seems to matter is that these are our traditional assembly activities which we concluded from a rational, objective study of the Bible, and we will follow this formula until death do us part. Which forces us to ask, are we the Bride of Christ or are we married to a formula?

Having two songs, a prayer, another song, the Lord's Supper, contribution, another song, the sermon, and an invitation song, has and never will be wrong, bad, or unscriptural. What is wrong, bad, and unscriptural is the belief that it MUST follow that formula or what is done is unacceptable to God. This makes the assembly a ritual, as mentioned before, but it has its roots in formula theology. It's the safe way; the rational way; and it's the tried and true way.

Rational religion also tends to rob us of the Spirit and the spirit. That's not a typographical error. Most of us were raised in churches where the slightest show of spirit could get one tarred and feathered and the mentioning of the Holy Spirit being present would cause widespread cardiac arrests. Even today, after all the battles about how the Holy Spirit dwells within the Christian, I still see tremors of fear cascade through the audience when I mention that we are led by the Spirit.

It's difficult to deal with the Holy Spirit on a totally rational level. It doesn't always make sense. That is why it has been avoided for so many years by so many Christians. It can't be reduced to a three- or five-step formula. It conjures up images of rolling in the aisles, handling snakes, and speaking pig Latin. It's far too mysterious and we are too enlightened to believe in the mysterious. So we tell folks to "repent, and . . . be baptized . . . for the forgiveness of your sins" and let them wonder (much later of course) what it means to "receive the gift of the Holy Spirit" (Acts 2:38).

What rational religion can't accept is that we don't have to understand everything in the Bible. It doesn't have to be logical. Love isn't always logical. Faith isn't always the natural conclusion of syllogistic reasoning. Faith is trust and assurance in what can't be seen, and sometimes, what can't be completely explained. I don't have to have a logical explanation, a theory, or an answer, but I do have to have faith.

The Bible says in Acts 2:38 that the Spirit was given to me as a gift. How does God do that? I don't know, but the Bible says it and that settles it.

The Bible says in Ephesians 5:18 that I need to be "filled with the Spirit." What happens then? Will I feel it? Will it take control of my life? Will I do strange things in the aisle on Sunday morning? I don't know! I do know that it's better than being filled with wine and it will make me want to sing. We could use some spiritual intoxication in the assembly.

The great comfort chapter, Romans 8, tells me that I must "walk according to the Spirit" (v. 4), set my mind on "things of the Spirit" (v. 5), be "in the Spirit" to please God (vv. 8-9), that the Spirit will "give life to your mortal bodies" (v. 11), that I am "led by the Spirit" (v. 14), that He "bears witness with our spirit that we are children of God" (v. 16), and that "the Spirit Himself intercedes for us with groanings too deep for words" (v. 26). I don't understand the how, when, why, or where of most of these concepts, but I'm glad it happens. I don't feel any tingly sensations going up and down my spine, I don't hear any whispering voices in the still of the night, and I haven't felt the urge to kiss a snake. Nevertheless, a Christian is Spirit filled and getting together is what Spirit-filled Christians do. That may frighten rational religionists, but it doesn't make it any less biblical.

I used to love preaching all those points about the Holy Spirit in Romans 8 and then forcefully declare, "I don't feel it, but the Bible says it and that settles it!" As we minister-types say, "That'll preach!" Then one day a brother asked me if I ever felt love. Before I could say "Of course, what a stupid question," he added, "What about joy, peace, kindness, or gentleness?" (Gal 5:22-23). I realized immediately what he was challenging me with. How could I say that I don't feel the Holy Spirit when I constantly feel the fruit of the Spirit? That doesn't mean that I have been overpowered and will soon be foaming at the mouth, but it does mean that the Spirit is present in my life — AND I MUST FEEL IT! Even in the assembly!

THE LITTLE "S"

The other problem with an overemphasis on the rational is that there is little or no room for the spirit, with the lower case "s." This is not to say that our traditional rational approach to religion is void of spirit. We just believe that the spirit can best be dealt with by keeping it bottled up inside rather than take the chance of doing something, or displaying something that doesn't look rational to all who may be present. For most of us, our rational religion means that we must be controlled, serious, meditative, and correct. This is usually seen as having a reverential attitude in the assembly. We've been raised to believe that it's a holy place, time, and occasion, and to be casual, open, and unrestrained is to be sacrilegious. All of that is in the Bible some place, isn't it?

Again, it is ironic that we insist on a logical approach to something that defies logic. The spirit is the soul, the heart, "the non-material ego in special relationship" with God.[8] Vine's *Expository Dictionary* gives some eighteen different ways that this word is used when it's not used as a pronoun referring to the Holy Spirit.[9] They all seem to say that the spirit is the eternal, inner essence of man; our conscience; our will; our reality; and most important of all, where God really dwells (if we let Him). While it's not a perfect word, it seems to me that our traditional habit of calling it "the heart" is about as accurate and simple as we can get. Since when did matters of the heart HAVE to be logical?

For too many years we have interpreted Jesus' declaration that "God is spirit, and those who worship Him must worship in spirit and truth" as meaning we must be accurate and sincere (John 4:24). While "truth" includes being accurate, "spirit" is more than being sincere. The spirit Jesus is calling for comes from deep within the heart. It boils and churns with thanksgiving, joy, praise, and love until it is free to explode in the presence of others who have had to restrain their feelings until they were with those who understood why they felt that way. Expressing the fruit of the Spirit is what the spirit was meant to do. It may not seem logical, but it certainly is biblical.

Sure it's difficult to judge the sincerity of one who displays the fruit of the Spirit, but not any more than it is to judge the sincerity of one who logically follows the accepted routines and rituals. Besides, we're not in the judging business. God knows both the Spirit and the spirit, and He won't make any mistakes.

Rational religion has caused us to have a deep distrust for emotionalism. After all, to be rational is to be objective, and emotions are far too subjective to coexist with the rational. As the younger folks say, "NOT!" There is absolutely no reason why a display of emotions cannot have a rational reason for happening. We have allowed our fear of being controlled by our emotions to create a head religion that has little room for the heart/spirit. When I was a teenager in the sixties, at Christian camps, rallies, and retreats, I experienced many mass revivals among my age group. There were times when a dynamic speaker would preach, touch every heart there, and have a hundred teenagers respond to the invitation to be baptized or spiritually restored. It was while attending a two-day retreat at Calloway Gardens in Georgia, in 1968, that one young man rededicated his life to God and made a commitment to preach the Gospel for the rest of his life. You either bought his book or had it given to you, because you're reading it now.

After these events, on several occasions, I remember hearing adults say things like, "Well, those kids were just responding to emotionalism. It won't stick!" Or they'd say something like, "Sure there were a lot of responses, but they all just got caught up in the spirit of the moment. You can't know enough to become a Christian and stay a Christian after hearing only one sermon!" On other occasions when young people would respond during the assembly and they would be broken and tearful, you could clearly see the discomfort of some brethren who felt it was far too emotional for their tastes.

While I am living proof that it "sticks," and the folks on the day of Pentecost in Acts 2 are proof that one short sermon can be more than enough, the real tragedy is the failure to understand that our emotions are just as integral a part of our faith as our intellect. Today the same kind of rational bad-mouthing of emotionalism is being leveled at new praise songs, hand clapping, hand raising, and calls to "greet one another" in the assembly.

A major reason why the assembly is a battleground today is because we can't agree on "the little s" spirit. We have no one to blame but ourselves! In my opinion, its modern day origin was our desire to meet the spiritual needs of our teens back in the '60s and '70s in order to stem the tide of young people who were deserting the church by droves. What was provided ultimately opened their eyes to new possibilities, which later caused them as young adults to demand more from the assembly than a logical liturgy of lifeless lists.

Churches hired Youth Ministers and developed active youth programs that were geared to that age group. Soon young people had special enthusiastic songs, dynamic speakers, and meaningful prayer times. The idea was to be relevant and fun, but still spiritually challenge them to commit to Jesus. At the same time, the youths were warned that these things "can't be done in the formal worship." When they asked why, the answer was never "Because the Bible tells us," but rather "The adults won't allow it." So it was accepted and assumed that the previous generation had worked it all out, and it must be God's will.

Year after year these young people graduated from high school and their youth group, and went off to college. At college some lost their faith and others developed an owned faith. When they asked "Why can't we do these things in the formal worship?" their professors either made it clear that it was tradition or they told them to search the Scriptures for themselves and find the answer. These young adults were brought up on the Bible and it didn't take them long to discover that the Bible really doesn't even address the subject.

After graduating from college, they got jobs, got married, started their families, and became part of the adult church. The joy and enthusiasm of their college and youth ministry days had ended. The adult church prayed and wailed about the declining church attendance, preached and cheered about church growth, but made it clear that it had to happen without changing anything. The answer to "why," which now came from their elders, was "It will upset some people and they will leave. So we just can't allow it."

For a while the new generation found fulfillment in providing for the spiritual needs of their young children. They threw themselves into Bible Hour, Children's Worship, Joy Buses, and VBS. For several years they were too busy serving to fight about the assembly. But then their kids became part of the Youth Group. Then their kids started asking "why." There was no loyalty to a pre-WW2 worship format and the rational religion of the past, but there was a fierce loyalty to the Word, the Restoration Plea, and the future of their children. So, the battle was joined.

Much has been written about the Baby Boomers and the Baby Busters, and their different perspective of what the church ought to be and do. I believe the bottom line is — the post-war generations have rejected the rational-only religion of the past generations and they seek a more balanced heart-and-head religion.

DISCUSSION QUESTIONS

1. What are some of the spiritual things that you once thought you fully understood, but in retrospect you now know you didn't fully understand?

2. Does it bother you to see brethren upset and arguing over what they want in the assembly?

3. Is it wrong to want predictability in the assembly? Why?

4. What are some of the problems with a strong emphasis on having a rational religion?

5. What are the dangers inherent in formula religion?

6. What would help your assembly to have more spirit? What would help it to have more Spirit?

7. When does emotionalism in the assembly become excessive?

8. Why do you think many people are fearful of emotionalism in the assembly?

CHAPTER 5
The Spirit of Timidity

3. **The Paranoid Church.** I have always felt sorry for the poor one-talent man. Haven't you? I guess I assumed that he had an inferiority complex because his master only gave him one talent. He had so little that he couldn't afford to lose it, so he buried it. Jesus said that when the master returned and demanded an accounting from the men he'd given five and two talents to, he was overjoyed with their success in doubling their talents. The poor one-talent man had nothing to show except the original talent. He had protected it, but he'd also failed to help it grow into something more. His explanation is one of the saddest verses in the Bible. He said, "I was afraid, and went away and hid your talent in the ground." The rest of his statement must have been said with a certain amount of glee. He added, ". . . see, you have what is yours" (Matt 25:14-30).

The one-talent man operated from an inadequate perspective and a false assumption. His inadequate perspective was fear. He said, "I was afraid." Was he afraid of his master, his potential failure, or his task? While fearing the Lord is the beginning of wisdom, we are expected to grow into a relationship of love. As far as failure or personal inadequacy is concerned, God never demanded success, but rather faithfulness. He promised that He would take care of the increase.

His false assumption was that the master wanted him to only return what he entrusted to him. If he had tried to increase what his master had given him but failed, and was only able to break even, it would have been a different story. God didn't give him the job of maintaining the status quo. He gave him a task to work on.

I see a clear parallel between this and our church assemblies. God gave us a task (a talent), and we responded to it just as the one-talent man did. We cry, "'I was afraid' of the truth being compromised, our purity being defiled, and our movement losing its uniqueness." So we became protectionists. Exclusive. Safe. Smug and intolerant. Undenominational sectarians. Fearful of new ideas, challenging interpretations, and change. We spoke where the Bible spoke and filled its silence with the security of traditions.

In fear we said "No" to changing our style of assembly. It wasn't a matter of Scripture, but rather, "Who knows what this will lead to?" We were afraid of false teaching, creeping liberalism, and looking too much like one of the denominations. It wasn't just "us against the world," but, "us against the religious world," and we had to be safe, peculiar, and distinctive at all cost. In short, we became a paranoid church, which later generations just didn't buy into.

Here are a few paranoid comments I have heard:

- ◆ "You can't use his book in your Bible class because he's not a member of the church."
- ◆ "If you don't require coats and ties for those who serve at the table, before you know it, someone will be up there in a swim suit."

- ◆ "If you're going to clap your hands to a song it won't be long until they'll be dancing in the aisles."
- ◆ "We can't raise our hands in the worship. People will think we're Pentecostal!"
- ◆ "Nope! We're not having that choir sing in this church. They had a bunch of liberals speaking at their last lectureship."
- ◆ "Women serve communion trays? Ya do that and they'll be in the pulpit in no time."
- ◆ "If all this 'Amening' keeps up, it won't be long before folks will want to 'Praise the Lord.'"
- ◆ "We can't make those folks mad. They'll leave and take their contribution with 'em."
- ◆ "If you move that communion table out, you might as well take the Word of God out with it."

Space and temperament won't permit a longer list, but these illustrate the language of fear that many of us grew up with, and still hear today. When did we forget that our distinctiveness is the love we have for one another? (John 13:35). When did we forget that faithfulness is seen in the Christlike compassion we show to "the least"? (Matt 25:31-40). When did we forget that "There is no fear in love; but perfect love casts out fear"? (1 John 4:18). Active love involves taking risks. This has nothing to do with compromising the truth, but everything to do with being what Jesus wants us to be. The problem is that fear doesn't take any risks. It only fortifies itself.

This brings us to the false assumption, not unlike what the one-talent man had, that God wants us to return to Him only what He gave us to begin with. When the Master returns, we visualize ourselves with a sparkle in our eye and a wide display of pearly whites showing as we present to Jesus His church and say, ". . . see, you have what is yours." Because we have protected it against false teachers and those who speak "the language of Ashdod," and because we reburied the Treasure, polished the Pearl, and sharpened the Sword, we think He will be pleased with His baby Bride. I wonder if Jesus will raise His voice and say:

So shall My word be which goes forth from My mouth; It shall not return to Me empty, Without accomplishing what I desire, And without succeeding in the matter for which I sent it. Isaiah 55:11

Somewhere along the way we stopped being "ambassadors for Christ" and became janitors of the status quo. Not only were all of our biblical interpretations infallible, but our established worship order became the law by which all others were to be judged. We took pride in being "steadfast, [and] immovable" like Paul told the Corinthians to be (1 Cor 15:58). That steadfastness and immovability wasn't only applied to The Truth, but our tried and true traditions. Maintaining "the old paths" was THE work of the church. It mattered little that the same verse in the Bible that told us to be steadfast and immovable also said, ". . . always abounding in the work of the Lord, knowing that your toil is not in vain in the Lord."

Christians must be unbending and beyond compromise concerning the Gospel of Jesus Christ, but we have been called to "abound" in His work; to bear fruit; to make disciples; to love the unlovely; to go unto all the world; to make known to the world the manifold wisdom of God; to work out our salvation with fear and trembling; to be faithful unto death; to walk in the Light; to love one another; to grow in the grace and knowledge of our Lord and Savior Jesus Christ; and . . . you know the list! While the Truth must never change, He wants us to grow and multiply to the extent that the Bride He returns to get is nothing like the one He started two thousand years ago. He expects (He actually demands) spiritual maturity and numerical growth.

It's a tough pill to swallow, but what does it profit a man if he maintains a 1940 assembly style but loses succeeding generations? I have brethren who tenaciously withstand any attempt to change an assembly tradition (not Scripture), even though they have grown children, my age, who haven't set foot in a church building since they left home. Years earlier, their children couldn't deal with the inflexible, fear-filled, hardnosed, protectionist religion of their folks, and now they reject all religion. It didn't take too many years of going to Bible classes as a child before they started asking the "why" questions about the assembly. It also didn't take long for them to realize that Scripture was irrelevant, and maintaining the status quo was everything. Many became casualties on the battlefield of the assembly, and many others are still around but they're walking wounded. And — the battle goes on.

ARE WE THERE YET, DADDY?

4. **The Historical Restoration**. Believe it or not, there are prominent historians who have never heard of The Restoration Movement. When I was doing graduate work at George Mason University, one of my professors, who was a nationally known American History expert and a staunch Baptist, had never heard about the Restoration Movement until he read my research paper for his class. He was pleasantly surprised, and I was shocked. I had always been led to believe that it was one of the pivotal events of our country's history. He was even more surprised when I told him that it was still going on.

Actually, I should have told him that "in theory" it's still going on. The call to be simply and only New Testament Christians, to go back to the Bible and be no more or less than they were, had its origins in that great 18th Century movement, but it didn't end in the 19th Century, or reach fulfillment in the 20th Century. It was a commitment to dig for the truth, keep learning, growing, and changing when we discovered something new. Unfortunately, many believe, or at least act as if all there is to restoring New Testament Christianity has been discovered and adopted. The attitude is, "We've arrived and we have it all figured out."

I grew up hearing preachers say, "We follow only the Bible. We encourage you to examine what we do, and if you can show us in the Bible where we are leaving something out or doing something wrong, we'll change and conform to the Word." That was so comforting to me when I was young. It not only spoke to our loyalty to God's message, but it spoke to our open-mindedness. It said to me that we are all **in the process** of becoming what God wants us to be. So I preached the same thing.

It wasn't long before I discovered how dishonest that statement was. We all held a smug belief that there was nothing that we had left out and there couldn't possibly be something that we were doing wrong. What we really should have said was, "If you believe that we are doing something wrong, we'd be happy to sign a debate proposition, have a public discussion of our soundness, and show you the error of your ways."

We really believed that we had restored all of New Testament Christianity and there was nothing left to be restored. Many still believe that today.

Again, I see a sad irony in this. All of our Bible teachers, who were pre-WW2 Christians, did such a good job of teaching us the principles of the Restoration that today many of us are screaming for a renewal of those principles. The goal is to be like they were in the New Testament, not like they were in 1850 or 1950. The insistence on following cultural traditions and religious rituals violates the very heart of that goal. It's not that the traditional assembly style is wrong, but it is the indefensible attitude that it is equal to and as important as those principles which has created the battle that rages across the nation today.

What exacerbates the problem even more than the attitude that "we've arrived" is the attitude that "our traditions are scriptural and your new ideas are unscriptural." Most of the time the battle isn't over Scripture; it's over preferences. It's one thing to lovingly tell a brother that his idea for the assembly is good, but probably not something we choose to do, and it's another to label him, condemn him, and tell him he's unbiblical.

In a recent congregational survey about the assembly, a large group of older Christians actually marked "raising hands" and "kneeling" during the assembly as unscriptural. The fact is that both of these are very scriptural and not just preferences, but they were so against them that in fear they decided to "vote" to keep them out of the assembly. When Scriptures aren't ignored, often they are just abused and used out of context. And all of this by brethren who have restored New Testament Christianity?

The Restoration Plea declared that "where the Bible is silent, we are silent," but there is more said about the silence than was ever said about the spoken Word. To some members the silence of the Bible means freedom, but to others it means "do it the way we've always done it."

There are nine verses in the New Testament that tell of Christians singing, or admonish Christians to sing. How is it we know so much about what was never said? Song books, types of songs, rhythms, words, how many song leaders, the number to be sung, invitation songs, how many must sing at a time, sound systems, clapping or toe tapping, whether or not songs were sung during communion, and what a big difference the closing prayer makes in terms of what can be sung, are just a few of the things that brethren have the inside scoop on even though the Bible is silent on them.

The Bible tells us almost nothing about what they did during the Lord's Supper. It tells us what kind of heart to have, the purpose of it, and what's supposed to be used, but many brethren just know there's Scripture for a Communion Table, trays, cover cloths, serving from the front, silence, no singing, and to break really means to pinch.

Is there Scripture for having pews, wearing suits and ties, thirty-minute sermons, invitations, reverential atmosphere, a song leader, a song book, a Sunday evening assembly, announcements, finishing by noon, and only allowing the song leader to have a microphone? People really and truly don't want to hear that these things are not in the New Testament and therefore not part of the Restoration.

Is it a surprise to anyone that several generations have come along who realize this and see the inconsistency of saying, "We've arrived?" The whole foundation of the Restoration Movement was a commitment to a consistent interpretation and application of God's Word. We can't pick and choose what we want from the Word as if it were some spiritual cafeteria. Honesty demands that we weed out inconsistencies. Love for the Word means that we are "handling accurately the word of truth" (2 Tim 2:15). Restoration means that we are constantly seeking to better emulate that first century church. To say we are when we clearly are not, well, it could cause a battle.

We can combine the last two reasons why the assembly is a battleground and say that many fear restoration. Restoration is never static. Restoration is constant change as we endeavor to be a more Christlike body. Many treasure security, dependability, and comfort more than they do the challenge to "be transformed by the renewing of [their] mind" (Rom 12:2). Those who want more in their assemblies are "liberals" and "change agents." Those who call for a rethinking of Scripture are charged with having a "new hermeneutic." A call for more restoration is a call to "fix what ain't broke."

The irony is that fear is timidity. Fear is insecurity. Fear is crippling and powerless. Fear despises restoration and inhibits real New Testament Christianity. As Paul said, "For God has not given us a spirit of timidity, but of power and love and discipline" (2 Tim 1:7). So in this battle over the assembly, who's right?

"IF IT FEELS GOOD, DO IT!"

5. **Selfishness**. He looked out his palace window and said, "I want that." It wasn't a beautiful woman or custom-built chariot that Ahab coveted, but rather a vineyard. Being the king of Samaria, he was used to getting what he wanted. So he approached the owner of the vineyard, a man named Naboth, and made his offer. Ahab's reasons for wanting it were valid. The property was close and he wanted a vegetable garden planted there. He offered Naboth a choice between another "better" vineyard somewhere else or cold hard cash.

Everything seemed reasonable until Naboth said, "Thanks but no thanks." It was a family inheritance, and he wasn't going to sell it for any reason or price. He actually said "No" to a king, who never had anyone say no to him. Listen to Ahab's reaction,

> So Ahab came into his house sullen and vexed because of the word which Naboth the Jezreelite had spoken to him; for he said, "I will not give you the inheritance of my fathers." And he lay down on his bed and turned away his face and ate no food" (1 Kgs 21:4).

Anyone who has ever had a two-year-old will recognize this behavior. It's called a temper tantrum, accompanied by severe pouting. I wish that were all it was, but as you know, his wife conspired to "fix things" by having Naboth falsely accused of blasphemy and disloyalty, which led to him being stoned to death. Following Naboth's death, Ahab simply took possession of the vineyard.

A Christian was sitting in his palace pew, watching things being done "decently and in order" — the right way, like it has always been done since he was a kid — and he said, "I want that!" But then something was done differently. A change took place. It was something new and undoubtedly unscriptural, and he gasped in shock. The rest of the time he sat with arms folded, lips tight, and eyes squinting. He was "sullen and vexed" and he vowed to get that traditional vineyard back no matter what the cost.

Another Christian was sitting in his palace pew wondering why things were so boring and predictable. "Why can't we do something different," he growled under his breath, "Something uplifting and new." He thought about the church across town that sang upbeat songs, used a Praise Team, and actually had "testimonials" from members. He thought, "I want that." But it wouldn't happen at his church. So he folded his arms, sighed loudly, and looked with scorn on "the old folks" who always got their way. He was "sullen and vexed" and he vowed to change things no matter who got hurt in the process.

One reason why the assembly is a battleground is because too many of us act more like Ahab than Jesus Christ. We need to remember who the vineyard belongs to.

This is where the finger pointing stops. The assembly has become a battleground, not because of "you traditionalists" or because of "you progressives," but because of US. The spirit of intolerance is an uncomely badge that must be pinned on the breast of every person who is "sullen and vexed" because they can't get what they want in the assembly. The selfish spirit of "I want" has divided churches, hurt brethren with verbal stones, and pushed Jesus aside as the owner. One of the most deplorable things to see happen today is brethren being un-Christlike about Christ's church. The name-calling, the generalizing, the labeling, and the judging have made us look more like a spoiled king than the King of Kings.

How did we get so insensitive, uncaring, and intolerant? We stopped breaking bread! We stopped getting close, building relationships, and emphasizing togetherness, and keyed in on having a correct, formal worship service. This will be discussed more later, but we stopped communicating, and when you don't communicate you speculate. A "hi" "bye" with a handshake in between doesn't build "unity of the Spirit." Since we don't know each other and understand one another's needs, it's easy to assume that something is wrong with you when you don't want what I want. We rob ourselves of the joy of sacrificing for the sake of a loved one, and what should have been the developing of the mind of Christ became the attitude of "my way or no way."

How did we get to be this way? I believe that because of our cultural and historical religious background, the assembly changed from a breaking of bread togetherness event to a formal worship. That formalism spawned a spectator mentality on the part of members, which caused us to start watching and judging everything that happened. The assembly went from being a blessing to an obligation and attendance became synonymous with faithfulness. Once one thought of himself as "a faithful member," one had the right, yea verily, the responsibility to assess the scriptural soundness and the appropriateness of what took place. This in turn gave rise to the judgmental monsters of performance and preference.

Most of us have spent our religious life sitting in the assembly like the proverbial "bump on a log." Instead of internalizing, examining ourselves, and seeking to edify others, we sat in judgment of the assembly leaders. We started mentally grading their performance. At the conclusion of the assembly/show we spent our trip home in the car and most of our Sunday dinner criticizing the performance.

We've all heard the joke about the family driving home from church, and the mom and dad fussed about how bad the sermon, the singing, and the communion comments were. Finally the youngest son in the back seat proclaimed, "Well, I thought it was pretty good entertainment for a dollar!" While we laugh at the joke, we all see the truth hidden in the humor.

As a preacher, I have always been amazed by the varied complaints of members. Surprisingly, I have heard far more complaints about incidentals than I have about doctrine. I've heard gripes about having my hands in my pocket, taking my coat off when I got too warm, not wearing a tie, sermon length, picking on people, having a hidden agenda, and not offering the entire plan of salvation during my invitation, just to name a few.

The poor song leader gets butchered by somebody no matter what he does. He picked the wrong kind of songs, led them too fast or too slow, had too many or not enough, talked too much or not enough, moved too much or not enough, pitched it too high or too low, and generally "didn't meet my needs."

I have often thought of the assembly audience as Olympic judges. I can almost see the stack of score cards on their laps and visualize that after each event in the assembly, each person would hold up the score that depicted the grade they would give for it. The problem would be, aside from the un-Christlike judgmental nature of the whole thing, that it would be a no-win situation. Because everything is based on personal preference, every event would receive everything from 0.0 to a perfect 10.0. What one person would like, another would dislike.

Intolerance reigns in the assembly because it stopped being a "one another" experience and became a "please me" event. Whether complaints come from a defense of traditions or a defense of freedom, the practice of coming into the assembly, sitting down, and demanding that others do something to make us feel good is selfish and ungodly. Until we all learn that we come together to do something special for someone else, and through our obedience worship God, the assembly will continue to be a battleground and the war will be unwinnable.

DISCUSSION QUESTIONS

1. In what ways have we become a paranoid church?
2. Have we completely restored New Testament Christianity?
3. Are there any Ahabs in the church today?
4. Why are "performance and preference" monsters of the assembly?
5. Why is there so much intolerance about the assembly among brethren?

CHAPTER 6
Dishwashers Anonymous

6. **Preeminence of the Assembly**. All the stories and events in the Bible are important and profitable when studied, but some seem to speak to us with timeless truths, and they never become trite or overused. The story of Jesus visiting the home of Mary and Martha is just such a story. The lessons that spring forth from it are powerful, relevant, and convicting.

According to the Luke 10 account, Martha invited Jesus into their home for dinner. She proceeded to be "distracted with all her preparations" while her sister Mary sat at the feet of Jesus drinking in every word He uttered. You can almost see the frustration building as she worked and Mary never lifted a finger to help. As Martha got angrier, she probably acted like we would and began clanging pots and pans together and banging them on the kitchen counter, hoping that Mary would get the hint. Finally she marched into the room where they were sitting and showed that she was clearly just as miffed at Jesus as she was at Mary. She said, "Lord, do You not care that my sister has left me to do all the serving alone? Then tell her to help me." After all, He was the Master and Mary was the servant, but she wasn't doing any serving.

Jesus probably smiled when He said, "Martha, Martha, you are worried and bothered about so many things; but only a few things are necessary, really only one, for Mary has chosen the good part, which shall not be taken away from her" (Luke 10:38-42).

His one sentence response spoke volumes about priorities. Why would anyone waste time whipping up a favorite recipe when the Bread of Life was sitting in their living room? Food is not totally unimportant, but when compared to the surpassing presence of Jesus Christ, it is certainly secondary.

When you have company for dinner, what is more important, the guests or the dinner? Is food preparation or washing dishes a higher priority than hospitality? I know folks who would quickly declare that the guests come first, but when you are in their home their conscientious work habits would seem to say otherwise. And they are good habits! People admire those who have a strong work ethic, who are industrious, and who want everything done right. But what is the point of the get-together? Food? Impressing guests? Building a relationship? It all comes down to priorities.

Because of our singular focus on the Christian assembly throughout the years, we have elevated a simple edification tool to the most import spiritual activity a Christian must participate in. There is no biblical justification for making the assembly such a preeminent Christian activity. It's important, like food and dishwashing, but the "really only one" necessary part is a day by day walk with Jesus.

As I mentioned in *Spilt Grape Juice*, we have a religion of the assembly. Being a Christian is synonymous with "going to church," and attendance is used as the primary quality for judging faithfulness.[10] For many it is the sum total of all the spiritual training, nourishment, and guidance they get, or want, the entire week. It's essential to salvation, a commandment from God, and the only place "real worship" takes place. If you are not there, you miss a chance to be with Jesus, encounter God, and find out who will be in heaven with you. You should be at all three weekly services, but the Sunday morning is the primary assembly. It's the formal worship. It's the one where the Lord's Table is set, and you must plan to stay, pray, and pay.

The assembly is a battlefield today because we created a monster that has now turned on its creator. Plenty of folks will vehemently disagree and say we've never said these things, but our actions, our traditions, and our legalistic approach to the assembly speak louder than all the false talk about the assembly being a matter of the heart.

By making the assembly preeminent, we created a recipe for problems. Since it is SO important and SO essential, and since it is the focal point of our religion, everyone has high expectations for what it must accomplish in their lives. It can't be all things to all people! It can't, and was never intended to, meet every need of every Christian. But since it's "all there is," and "all we really need," it can't avoid being a source of serious conflict. After all, we all know that Sunday is the day of worship, the Sunday morning assembly the hour of worship, and the church building the place of worship. So what other choice do we have?

Where is the biblical authority for the preeminence of the assembly? We can't even find a complete example of an entire assembly in the New Testament. What we know and have come to think of as chiseled in stone, has been pieced together like a jigsaw puzzle from selected verses throughout the Bible. Does that mean our conclusions are wrong? I'm not saying they are, but I am saying that the assembly was not nearly as much the focus of Christianity

81

in the New Testament as we have traditionally made it. There are precious few passages that deal with the assembly, and the ones that do are very matter-of-fact about the whole thing. Getting together is just what Christians do!

Why are the "day to day" New Testament examples less important than the "first day of the week" examples? Why is the word "worship" never used in the New Testament about Christians in connection with the assembly? What verse in the New Testament shows us that the New Testament Christians understood that a block of time on Sunday was the most important spiritual time for them? Even the overused admonition in Hebrews 10:25 for us to "not forsake our own assembling together" is merely talking about Christians getting together in order to encourage one another. Which assembly was the writer talking about? All of them!

The Christian assembly is merely one of the tools from God for spiritual growth. It's important, but not more than personal prayer, study, and meditation. It's not any more important than Bible classes, small groups, ministries, fellowships, acts of service, evangelism, or walking in the light any day or time of the week. We made the assembly the most important thing a member can participate in and then are surprised when we regularly get nothing else from them. What was meant to be the icing on the cake has become the whole cake.

Did you ever notice that those members who are very involved in several works and ministries do the least amount of complaining about the assembly? That's not always true of course, because many feel it's their mission in life to complain, but most of the folks who find fulfillment in service, who are growing and becoming more Christlike, don't HAVE to have all their needs filled in the assembly. Maybe we need to start elevating other spiritual opportunities and then the assembly will stop being the center of our religious world, and our battle.

As hard as it is to believe, there are things more important than the assembly. I have mentioned several examples and there are many more. Maybe we need to deal with the question of who decides what may be more important than the assembly?

Think about Jesus and His battles with the Pharisees over the Sabbath day and what really was important. One of these startling stories was the time Jesus healed a man who had been crippled from birth. He purposely did it on the Sabbath to make a statement about His power, His authority, and His compassion. All the Pharisees saw was a man violating the Sabbath by carrying his bed. (See John 5:1-17.) Another time Jesus went right into the synagogue on the Sabbath and healed a man's withered hand. (See Mark 3:1-6.) Then there was the woman who had been sick for eighteen years and was bent double by the illness, and Jesus placed His hand on her and healed her. (See Luke 13:10-17.) During some of these healings, and others, Jesus pointed out the inconsistency of the Pharisees in that they would rescue an ox or a sheep that had fallen in a well on the Sabbath, but they wouldn't show compassion and want someone healed on the same day. He was the "Lord of the Sabbath" and the Lord's work of love always came first.

It seems clear to me we must conclude that doing the Lord's work may involve doing something that, at least for the moment, is more important than the assembly. Who decides? Jesus must be the final judge, and The Judge has told us that compassion is the first order of business for His followers. Satan loves it when we automatically assume if a brother is absent from the assembly he must be "forsaking" it. He could be taking care of the compassion that the Priest and Levite avoided by walking by on the other side of the road. (See Luke 10:30-37.)

Please do not conclude that the assembly is unimportant. God wants His people to be together. Few things are more clearly taught in the New Testament. There is nothing, however, that even remotely hints at the preeminence we have given to the assembly. It's not the most important or the least important thing Christians do. It is something Christians do, but not THE THING Christians do.

I long to hear brethren arguing about saving souls, visiting hospitals, and feeding the hungry instead of bickering about what we want in the assembly. Christlike folks who are busy caring "for the least of these" haven't got time to wail and gnash their teeth about what's happening or not happening in the assembly, and they won't be wailing or gnashing their teeth in the life to come, either. How are we going to explain to Jesus why we focused so much time and energy on the assembly while our neighbors were dying in sin? We've been too busy fighting battles that should never have been fought.

WHEN THE ROOSTER CALLS

7. **The Forgotten Jesus**. I was still rubbing the sleep from my eyes in the pre-dawn darkness when I arrived at my previously selected tree. It was a large oak that was straight and had no branches on its lower half to get in the way of my climbing tree stand. I quickly and quietly attached the hand climber and the platform to the tree. I was so excited about bowhunting for deer and having my tree stand in just the right place that I had to force myself to take my time and think safety first.

A climbing tree stand works on the simple principle of wedging. A blade on the backside of the tree bites into the bark and has bracing on either side of the tree that attaches to a front bar which bites into the tree from the front. This creates a wedge in the tree. The hand climber is used to pull up on, while the platform, with feet secured in elastic footholders, is pulled up and wedged into place. You can then stand on the platform, slide the hand climber up, and start all over again. Each time you rise about two feet up the tree. It takes a lot of coordination and a lot of stomach muscles.

As I reached a height of about fifteen feet, I secured the platform with bungee cords and moved the hand climber out of the way. I then removed my backpack, hung it on a tree limb, and then took in the view I had of the surrounding terrain. It was a beautiful morning. The sky was turning pink in the east giving me enough light to see the crossing deer trails just twenty yards from my stand. The perfect distance for a bow shot. I could see the fall colors of the leaves begin to brighten up, and as I looked over the leaf-covered ground, I could see my bow laying at the base of the tree with my pull-up rope neatly coiled beside it — the rope I had forgotten to attach to my belt before the arduous climb up the tree.

While people may argue about what they enjoy most about hunting, I think it's safe to say that a bow is an essential part of bowhunting. In fact, without the bow one is a spectator and not a participator. The sunrise is still spectacular and the flora and fauna are still breath-taking, but without the bow you're just not bowhunting.

Jesus is THE reason why we assemble together as Christians. We belong to Him, we are married to Him, we are remembering Him, He binds us together, we put on His mind, and for us "to live is Christ." The church is the body of Christ! He is the head over all things! We are growing to be like Him! We are being changed into His likeness from one degree of glory to another! He is the One we aim to please! So — where is He on Sunday morning?

Too many of us climb into our pew stand on Sunday morning and start hunting happiness, security, comfort, change or tradition, orderliness, reverence, a shot in the arm, and a taste of heaven, only to miss it all because we didn't stay attached to Jesus. While we argue about what we enjoy most, we leave out the most essential part — Jesus.

The Bible does not teach that there is a special presence of Jesus in the assembly. Since each one of us has the spirit of Christ, isn't it safe to say that there is more of the spirit of Christ present when we are together than when we are alone? The whole point of getting together is edification. What is edification if it isn't building one another up in Jesus? The idea is that when Christians rub shoulders with one another, a little bit of Jesus is supposed to rub off on one another and we all leave with a little more of Him than when we got there.

We haven't got time for Jesus in our assembly because we've got to get those "five acts" accomplished. I know a preacher who was fired because he preached too much from the Gospels and not enough from the Epistles of Paul. I know another preacher who was told to never preach about traditions, which immediately removed about a third of Jesus' teachings as sermon material. It's not surprising then that church folks don't know Jesus. They know the plan of salvation but not the One who paid the price for the plan. Many of our folks wouldn't even know where to begin if they had to do like Philip did in Acts 8 when he "opened his mouth, and beginning from this Scripture he preached Jesus to him" (Acts 8:35).

The simple fact that brethren are arguing about what style the assembly should be is a sad indictment of a lost focus on Jesus. We scream, "But I know what I want," and He tells us to go the second mile, just as if we really wanted to. We want to feel good in the assembly, and He says that good feelings come from being pure of heart, meek, a peacemaker, and suffering for righteousness' sake. We carry mental scorecards into the assembly, but He says, "Do not judge lest you be judged yourselves." Some even threaten to withhold their contribution if the assembly doesn't follow their will, but Jesus tells us, "where your treasure is, there will your heart be also." We insist that everyone do for us, but He says, "whatever you want others to do for you, do so for them." When Jesus is left out of the assembly, everything gets twisted around.[11]

I've held off long enough. It's time to use it. I am referring to the consummate passage in the New Testament in regard to our attitudes about the assembly. The principles in this passage are the reason why the Jerusalem church in Acts 2 was so appealing and the absence of these principles are why the church in Corinth had so many problems. This is the hub, the heart, and the bow. This is the solution to all your congregational problems. If every member of your church will commit to this you will never argue again about what should take place in your assembly. Put on your spiritual seat belt and open your heart to this:

> . . . lay aside every encumbrance, and the sin which so easily entangles us, and let us run with endurance the race that is set before us, **fixing our eyes on Jesus, the author and perfecter of faith**, who for the joy set before Him endured the cross, despising the shame, and has sat down at the right hand of the throne of God.
>
> For **consider Him who has endured** such hostility by sinners against Himself, so that you may not grow weary and lose heart (Heb 12:1-3, emphasis added).

Can you imagine what an impact that could have on our assembly? There's a boatload of stuff we need to "lay aside." Things that slow us down, get in the way, and distract us from our goal. And there is a race that we must run — a race we began when we gave our lives to Jesus, and we must not slow down or quit. The only way to accomplish this is to **fix our eyes on Jesus**. When we start feeling sorry for ourselves, **consider Him** who suffered far more than any of us will ever have to endure. The Christian who is focused on Jesus will not see changes or no changes in the assembly as something worthy of two seconds of anxiety. It's only when we lose our focus that the assembly becomes a battleground.

It is impossible to separate Jesus from His message. He is the Word and the Word is Jesus. To reject His message is to reject Him. Among other things, that should change the way we look at Peter's denials of Christ. Jesus had told Peter that he'd deny Him three times before the cock would crow the next morning, but Peter refused to believe it. As you know, Peter was challenged three times about his association with the Nazarene, and each time he forcefully denied any relationship with Jesus at all.

When that rooster crowed, it must have cut through the morning darkness and into Peter's heart like a lightning bolt. He instantly knew that he'd denied Jesus. The conviction sliced his soul and he wept out loud like a grief-stricken widow. The pain of his failure became an open wound that could only be healed by the Great Physician Himself.

Aren't you glad that rooster isn't in our assemblies today? If he crowed every time one of us denied Jesus through ignoring His word, how often would he crow? Every time we bring out our scorecard? Every time we scowl, frown, gripe, criticize, judge, corner an elder, shake our heads, assign blame, send nasty notes, refuse to sing "that type of song," get angry, or in any way are un-Christlike? What do you think? Would the rooster crowing drown out the rest of the assembly? In my opinion — no! There are too many good, loving Christians sitting in your assembly. There are a few, however, on both sides of every issue, who need to hear the caustic convicting crow of the rooster. We all need to hear it occasionally, just to remember to keep our eyes **fixed on Jesus.**

DISCUSSION QUESTIONS

1. How did the assembly become the center of our religious life?

2. Why is it that by making the assembly so important "we created a recipe for problems"?

3. What are some things that may be more important than the assembly?

4. Is there a special presence of Jesus in the assembly?

5. How much of your assembly time is spent focusing on Jesus?

CHAPTER 7
"If It Walks Like a Duck . . . ."

In the fall, my associate minister and I rise up early in the morning on our day off and drive to our hunting spot just outside of the booming metropolis of Hico, Texas. The brethren think we are fanatical bowhunters, but the real reason we make the 170-mile round trip is to eat a late breakfast at the famous Koffee Kup Restaurant in downtown Hico. It is known for its homemade pies, but I am partial to their oversized doughnuts. Just the thing to top off a huge ham and eggs breakfast.

As we came out of the Koffee Kup one morning and approached my Plymouth Grand Voyager minivan, I froze in horror. The right front tire on my van, one of four almost brand-new tires, was badly worn on the outside edge. I couldn't believe it! I felt the tire to see if I were dreaming, but it was very real. I circled the vehicle and checked the other three tires, but they looked in good condition. "How could that happen?" I asked my trusted partner. "These barely have five thousand miles on 'em!" He was as shocked as I. He suggested, "Maybe you need a front-end alignment."

In disgust, I walked to the driver's side and punched the unlock button on my key chain, but nothing happened. The door lock didn't pop up like it was supposed to. I hit it again and again. Nothing! "Oh great," I muttered. "Now the automatic door lock won't work!" How could such a great day go sour so quickly?

Just as I started to put the key in the door of my white minivan, I looked through the window and noticed the blue interior. Now I was really dumbfounded. My van has a grey interior! It must have been the loss of sleep or the overindulgence in the Koffee Kup, because it took several seconds for the proverbial "ton of bricks" to land on my head. Boy did I feel stupid when it did! This was not Mike Root's van! My nearly identical van was parked three spaces further out, and even at that distance I could see that the tires were just fine. I didn't even want to think about the folks in the restaurant, on the other side of the glass door, who had been watching our inspection. The owner might have been one of those spectators, and I could just imagine his amazement over his plain white van attracting such close scrutiny. It's not like it was a Corvette or a Rolls Royce.

Not only had my judgments been wrong, but because of that all my anger and anxiety were totally misplaced. It was the right model, the right color, and even in my usual parking space, but it just wasn't what I thought it was — my vehicle. I was humbled by my failure to thoroughly investigate before reaching my conclusions, and I was shocked that I could be so emotional about something that was so wrong.

I have seen nothing that Christians exhibit more passion for than the worship assembly. Benevolence, evangelism, youth work, mission work, and service are, at best, a distant second in practice if not theory. It seems logical to most that just as the tabernacle worship and the temple worship of the Old Covenant seemed to be the center of their religion, Sunday morning church worship must be the center of our religion. To question that is heretical, threatening, and the quickest way to make church folks angry. Nevertheless, our traditional thinking on worship is like that van outside the Koffee Kup Restaurant. It's the style we like, it's the color we like, it has the right name on it, and it has everything we are used to having, so therefore it must be WORSHIP. The problem is that it can't take us anywhere because it's not the one God gave us the pink slip for. We've been kicking tires and pushing buttons and nothing's been happening except for a lot of arguing about "why."

Many are looking at the wrong vehicle because they are looking at the Old Testament. At times we are terribly inconsistent with our theology. A fundamental element of restoring New Testament Christianity is the clear biblical teaching that the Old Law is not in force any more. Paul said that just as a woman whose husband dies is free to marry another, ". . . you also were made to die to the Law through the body of Christ, that you might be joined to another, to Him who was raised from the dead, that we might bear fruit for God" (Rom 7:4). In Galatians 3 he compared the Law to a tutor, "But now that faith has come, we are no longer under a tutor" (Gal 3:25). He was even more forceful in Colossians 2 when he described the Old Law as being "canceled" by Jesus because "He has taken it out of the way, having nailed it to the cross" (Col 2:14).

We use this argument to teach others that Christians don't keep the Sabbath, use incense, offer animal sacrifices, and have temples, priests, and religious festivals. Yet many see no problems with digging verses from the Old Testament to use as proof-texts for reverence in the assembly or why the assembly is "vertical" in that it's directed toward God. Every defense of traditional worship that I have seen is filled with passages of Scripture from Psalms, Proverbs, or the Prophets, and many times there's not a single mention of a New Testament verse.

Where's the New Testament principle that teaches what we sometimes sing? What do we mean when we sing "The Lord is in His Holy Temple?" What are members thinking as they harmonize on "We are standing on Holy ground?" I love those songs and others like them, but I have to do some mental gymnastics to give them a New Testament meaning when I sing them. Our doctrine says that the individual Christian is "the temple of the Holy Spirit," but our practice is temple worship.

I believe it's inconsistent to say, "Our theology of worship must come from the Old Testament." This is a blatant effort to justify formal or high church traditional practices. Worship is a component of the covenant relationship with God. When the covenant changes, everything changes, unless it is restated again in the new covenant.

In High School Bible class, almost thirty years ago, I had to memorize three verses that tell us what the Old Testament is for Christians. I've never forgotten it. Here they are:

> Romans 15:4 "For whatever was written in earlier times was written for our instruction, that through perseverance and the encouragement of the Scriptures we might have hope."
>
> 1 Corinthians 10:11 "Now these things happened to them as an example, and they were written for our instruction, upon whom the ends of the ages have come."
>
> Galatians 3:24 "Therefore the Law has become our tutor to lead us to Christ, that we may be justified by faith."

We read and study the Old Testament because it does provide examples and insights for us, but only to "lead us to Christ." In it we see God's dealings with His people, and we learn that God is totally consistent, while man is always inconsistent. God has not changed. He cannot change. But, the way He deals with mankind has changed with each covenant. At one time He had a covenant relationship with the family patriarchs, and He told them directly what He wanted them to do.

Later, He had a covenant established through Moses, and He required circumcision as a sign of acceptance. He developed a Law that detailed how they were to live, work, worship, and carry out His plans. It was impossible for anyone to perfectly keep the Law and thus be saved, but part of His plan was to show the need for grace.

Thus, in the New Covenant, we are saved by grace "through faith; and that not of yourselves, it is the gift of God; not as a result of works, that no one should boast." As His children, we don't just do good works, it's His intent "that we should walk in them" because of the change that has taken place in our hearts (Eph 2:8-10).

What He wants from man was stated clearly in the beginning and has been restated throughout the Bible and for every covenant. God wants us to love Him completely, with our heart, soul, mind, and strength. Moses, the Prophets, Jesus, Paul, James, and Peter all repeated the same thing — love God; it's the first and greatest commandment. But the Law couldn't do it. Because of man's imperfections, law doesn't foster love, it fosters legalism. While God wanted love and devotion, His people saw the Law as an external religion, and they consistently missed the matters of the heart. Still, it was preparing the way for a much more spiritually oriented covenant that would emphasize heartfelt faith.

In the Old Testament, God's people constantly missed the point of what God was really wanting from them. They continually separated obedience to the Law and a personal love for God. Their acts of worship became their religion and their love for law led them to elevate tradition to being equal to God's commands. As a result, all too often their worship was physical, external, and empty. This led to condemnations like Isaiah's in Isaiah 1:11-15:

> "What are your multiplied sacrifices to Me?"
> Says the Lord.
> "I have had enough of burnt offerings of rams,
> And the fat of fed cattle.
> And I take no pleasure in the blood of bulls, lambs,
>   or goats.
> When you come to appear before Me,
> Who requires of you this trampling of My courts?
> Bring your worthless offerings no longer,
> Incense is an abomination to Me.
> New moon and sabbath, the calling of assemblies —
> I cannot endure iniquity and the solemn assembly.
> I hate your new moon festivals and your appointed
>   feasts,
> They have become a burden to Me.
> I am weary of bearing them.
> So when you spread out your hands in prayer,
> I will hide My eyes from you,
> Yes, even though you multiply prayers,
> I will not listen.
> Your hands are covered with blood."

How could things get to the point where God hated acts of worship? They had separated worship from their lifestyles. They turned tools of spiritual growth into meaningless rituals. They felt religious because of all their worship activities, and then lived evil lives the rest of the time. What they needed to do was:

> Wash yourselves, make yourselves clean;
> Remove the evil of your deeds from My sight.
> Cease to do evil,
> Learn to do good;

Seek justice,
Reprove the ruthless;
Defend the orphan,
Plead for the widow. (vv. 16-17).

Similar things are seen throughout the writings of the prophets. Read Jeremiah's Temple Sermon in Jeremiah 7 where he condemns their inconsistencies. In Amos 5:21-24, the prophet rejects their festivals, solemn assemblies, offerings, songs, and music. He says, "Let justice roll down like waters and righteousness like an everlasting stream." God is not just saying that He wanted more sincerity and concentration during acts of worship. He wanted His people to love Him enough to be godly.

What we learn about worship in the Old Testament is that when God is localized, given a place where He dwells and can be approached, it's easy to assume that one can walk away from Him and leave Him there, separating one's religious life from one's secular life. So in the Old Testament we see the condemnation of rituals, the supremacy of faith, the call for compassion and mercy over assemblies and sacrifices, and above all, we see the need for a covenant of grace.

THE NEW COVENANT WORSHIP

In small groups or seminars I like to ask the question, "Where's the best place to worship?" I usually get answers like "on a mountain top" or "a sunrise service on a beach." I've heard every possible place from closets to stadiums. I usually tell about the worship service we had on the back porch of a friend's cabin in Red River, New Mexico, or the worship services at summer camp in the Chapel in the Woods, or even the times in college when we had our Sunday evening services on the bus coming back from some chorus trip. It always amazes me that no one ever mentions the church building, and no one ever mentions life.

I wonder how Jesus would answer that question. Would He assume that worship was a place, time, or event? Was He worshiping during the forty days and nights that He fasted on the mountain? Was He forsaking the assembly (or at least the synagogue)? Why is it that in His description of the Judgment, the only thing He mentions is benevolence and compassion, but never worship? (See Matt 25:31-46)

Actually, Jesus did answer that question. It wasn't asked by one of the Pharisees or other religious leaders of His day, but rather by a woman. And she wasn't your average Jewish lady either. You could say that she had three strikes against her. First, she was a woman, and in that culture, women were sometimes seen as nothing more than property, and a man certainly didn't talk to a female stranger. Secondly, she was a Samaritan, an outcast, a hated and unclean people for any self-respecting Jew. And finally, she was a sinner. Not just in the general sense, as in "all have sinned," but in an overt and widely known way, as in "living in sin."

We call her "the woman at the well" because we don't know her name, and we find great comfort in the fact that Jesus showed compassion on one whom most of the world labeled a "reject." He not only talked to her, but He had a deep theological discussion with her. As a part of this discussion He revealed a supernatural knowledge of her sinful living, and this caused her to quickly change the subject. She stated, "Our fathers worshiped in this mountain; and you people say that in Jerusalem is the place where men ought to worship" (John 4:20).

The hurt and divisiveness are obvious in the words "you people." She wanted to know if He was just like all the other Jewish people, who felt spiritually superior to everyone else, especially the Samaritans. So the question is clearly implied: "What do you have to say about where worship should take place?" She gave Him two choices, Samaria or Jerusalem, and He chose "None of the above."

The answer that Jesus gave her in John chapter 4 has been used by so many for so long as a proof-text for maintaining our traditional approach to worship that it may be impossible for some to truly see what Jesus is saying. Generally, we assume that what we are doing is "in spirit and in truth," and we use Jesus' imperative here to prove that if your worship assembly is not like ours, you are practicing false worship. We just know that Jesus is talking about the Sunday morning worship service when He answers this woman's question. That is not only taking His words out of context, but it's missing the whole point of what He is saying.

What Jesus is doing in this passage is setting the stage for the New Covenant approach to worship. The word that Jesus uses for worship is the Greek word *proskuneo*, which means "to bow down, kiss, and do obeisance to." Jesus says, "Woman, believe Me, an hour is coming when neither in this mountain, nor in Jerusalem, shall you worship the Father." It's not here yet, but soon you won't bow down and do obeisance in Jerusalem or anywhere else. That's not the kind of worship God wants anymore. For centuries that is exactly what had been going on in the Temple in Jerusalem, and people came by the thousands to bow down and do their obeisance in "The House of God." But Jesus says, "Not any longer."

Jesus continued,

"But an hour is coming, and now is, when the true worshipers shall worship the Father in spirit and truth; for such people the Father seeks to be His worshipers. God is spirit; and those who worship Him must worship in spirit and truth." (See John 4:7-30; especially vv. 23-24.)

Jesus has already declared that worship is no longer a place, and now He describes what God really wants from

His people. Notice again the reference to a change. "An hour is coming, and now is" refers to the coming of the New Covenant. It's close at hand, Jesus says, but not quite here yet. He knew that it wouldn't go into effect until after His death, but the use of "shall" is clearly future tense.

It also seems that "true worshipers" is used in contrast with those who worship the Father at a place, like Jerusalem or Samaria. One would assume that there were people in those places who worshiped from the heart with a sincere desire to obey God, but soon they wouldn't be the "true worshipers."

To completely understand the magnitude of what Jesus is calling for in this passage, we must understand three key subjects: spirit, truth, and worship.

One of the most profound statements in the New Testament is Jesus' declaration that "God is spirit." He didn't say that God was "a" spirit, but simply "spirit." He is not one of many, He is the embodiment of all that is spiritual. This is one of four emphatic descriptions of God in the New Testament. In 1 John 1:5, "God is light;" in 1 John 4:8 and 16, "God is love;" and in Hebrews 12:29, "our God is a consuming fire." All of these deal with the very nature of God and speak to things we must understand if we are to know Him and be like Him.

Jesus says that God is spirit in contrast to His being a place. He is not limited by location or time because He is spiritual. We cannot and must not place any physical restrictions on the Creator of Heaven and earth. This is a call for a radical change in our their thinking about God. Jesus is essentially telling them to remove any thinking about the tabernacle, the temple, the Holy Place, and the Holy of Holies out of their minds. He is the everywhere God who must be part of everything in their lives.

Several years later, long after the church had been established, Paul made the same point to the folks on Mars Hill. He said,

The God who made the world and all things in it, since He is Lord of heaven and earth, does not dwell in temples made with hands; neither is He served by human hands, as though He needed anything, since He Himself gives to all life and breath and all things . . . . He is not far from each one of us; for in Him we live and move and exist . . . (Acts 17:24-25, 27-28).

The connection with God was no longer a physical connection, but rather a spiritual connection. God's people are now spiritual Israel. His temple is the heart of every Christian. Each child of God is now a priest, with Jesus being the only great High Priest. There is no holy day, only a holy life and Jesus became the once-and-for-all sacrifice for sins. We no longer bow down and do obeisance at the temple to worship God, but we present our bodies as a "living sacrifice" to Him, and this is our acceptable worship.

This emphasis on a personal and spiritual connection with God is a fundamental element of the New Covenant. God wants a personal relationship with every heart that seeks Him. Our relationship with Him is not based on works but grace, and in love and gratitude we obey Him. Good works become the result of the relationship and not the basis for the relationship. This is a radical change from the way things were in the Old Covenant — not what He wanted in the Old, but the way things were.

Since God is spirit and not limited by time and space, the worship of God is not limited by time and space. The only requirements are that He be worshiped in spirit and truth. When Jesus said that "those who worship Him must worship Him in spirit and truth," He was not talking about the Christian assembly. He was talking about the heart of a child of God twenty-four hours a day, seven days a week.

The way this passage is usually interpreted comes from our traditional understanding that worship is what we do on Sunday. It is an unbiblical presupposition, but it is the only definition for worship that we have ever known. As a result, we are forced to make some wild assumptions. Since we have figured out what is supposed to take place in Sunday worship, we therefore have "the truth," and since God is spirit and we have His truth figured out, we must therefore have spirit too. Therefore, we worship God in spirit and truth. Those who disagree with us and do something different on Sunday are just not worshiping God in spirit and truth.

Anyone who thinks that Jesus was referring to "the five acts of worship" or doing things on Sunday in a "decent and orderly fashion" is sorely missing the point. He is actually trying to bring about an end to that kind of thinking.

The word "spirit" is not a technical term, nor should it be scary. It simply means spiritual. The word "truth," which includes spiritual absolutes, is really being used to describe the very nature of God as the embodiment of truth. He is truth, not just the proclaimer of truths. To worship Him in truth means that we must internalize Him. Our obedience must come from a heart-level honesty. Jesus purposely used words that were all inclusive and total-life oriented to both describe God and explain how He was to be worshiped. Both of these are words that capture the core of what God has always wanted from His people, and that is love. I believe that Jesus is literally saying, "In the new covenant you will no longer bow down to God at a special place or time, but you will bow down to Him with a heart that is spiritual, honest, and totally given to Him."

It is with this new understanding of worship that we must interpret all of the other passages in the New Testament that discuss worship. Any attempt to recreate a temple-type worship in the New Covenant is to violate this profound principle Jesus is describing to the woman at the well.

Before I move on to a more detailed study of New Testament worship, think about this: would Jesus' answer have been different if the woman's question had been, "Some people say that worship should be traditional, while others say that it should be contemporary; what do you think, Jesus?" The answer to that is so easy it's like bobbing for water — you can't miss.

DISCUSSION QUESTIONS

1. Why is it dangerous to use the Old Testament to define New Testament worship?

2. What things didn't change from the Old covenant to the New?

3. Where is the best place to worship?

4. What did Jesus say about the time and place for worship in John 4:21-24?

5. What does it mean to worship God in spirit and in truth?

6. When do we "bow down" and worship God?

SECTION THREE
Real Worship

CHAPTER 8
"It's in There Somewhere!"

As I walked past the boys' cabin I could hear the counselor having a little devotional talk with the young boys inside. It was a Christian summer camp, one that I had gone to as a kid, and now I was the recreation director as I prepared for my first year of college. I had been on my way to the camp kitchen to see if there were any leftovers I could sample, but I couldn't resist the urge to stand outside the cabin window and listen to what the counselor had to say to his boys.

He generally gave them a lesson on being responsible and not being afraid of hard work. He'd used a few passages of Scripture to encourage them. Then he said, "In the Bible, I'm not sure where but it's in there somewhere, it says that God helps those who help themselves." It was a nice little lesson, but it made me laugh to myself.

I had always been told that Benjamin Franklin made the statement "The Lord helps those who help themselves." It sounds like something from the Bible, but it is actually more the product of American thinking than it is biblical theology. After all, God constantly helps those who can't help themselves. That's what salvation is all about, not just somewhere, but in Romans 5:6 where Paul says, "For while we were still helpless, at the right time Christ died for the ungodly." Aren't you glad?

Like many people, the camp counselor was so sure that his quote came from the Bible that he just knew it was in there somewhere. Well, the truth is, it is not in there anywhere.

Everyone knows what Christian worship is, right? It is what we do on Sunday at the church building. We don't have to prove that with the Bible because **EVERYONE** already knows what it is. The traditional view of worship is so steeped in our history and culture that there is no need to check with the New Testament, we just know that it's in there somewhere.

Worship has been defined as the formal Sunday morning assembly for so many centuries that it long ago became a universal truth. It's beyond defending, beyond rethinking, and certainly beyond question. It is so universally accepted that even the scholars and theologians begin their examination on the subject with that presupposition. I have yet to find a definitive biblical argument for our traditional view of worship. We simply take care of that by reading the word "worship" into every New Testament discussion of the assembly to make up for its absence in the text.

Because of my interest in the subject of worship and because of my past writing about it, I have several shelves of books to use for my research. Without exception, even among the well-known scholars, they begin with the presupposition that worship is the Christian assembly. Let's be clear. According to the New Testament the Christian assembly is worship, but it is not THE worship. We may want to believe that the traditional/historical view of worship is in the New Testament somewhere, but the truth is it's not in there anywhere.

What you find when you start researching the subject is a virtual ignoring of the New Testament, the covenant changes, and the emphasis on living worship, and a free-wheeling use of Old Testament passages to help define worship as a place and a time. The usual approach to the subject begins with a definition of the English word "worship." You'll read, "The term comes into our modern speech from the Anglo-Saxon weorthscipe. This later developed into worthship, and then into worship. It means, 'to attribute worth' to an object. . . . To worship God is to ascribe to Him supreme worth, for He alone is worthy."[12]

Who can argue with this, and why would you want to? Especially when it is always followed by selected passages from Psalms about the greatness of God and the importance of praising Him. The New Testament exalts the greatness of God and there are plenty of passages that talk about us praising God! But where are the passages associating this with the Christian assembly? We just know they're in there somewhere, and if they're not, we will just add them on our own.

A good example of what I am referring to is found in the scholarly book by Dr. Robert Webber, *Worship Old and New*, which is used as a textbook at several Christian colleges. It's a wonderful historical study of worship, but look at the assumptions made as he defines worship. He writes:

> The community character of worship is particularly emphasized in the Eucharist. Here the whole church comes together (see 1 Cor.11:18, 33; 14:23; Ignatius, Letter to the Ephesians 13:1; Didache 14:1; Justin, 1 Apol.67). The term **comes together** was used as a technical word in the early church to describe the gathering of Christians for worship. It pointed to the indisputable character of public worship as something that the church does in community. The public worship of the church occurs only when "two or three come together in [Jesus'] name" (Matt.18:20).[13]

I do not use this quote to debate with or refute Dr. Webber, but rather as an example of our presuppositions about worship. In fairness to his book, he does give a much broader definition than this quote, but this reflects typical thinking and usage of some key Bible verses. First Corinthians 11:18 reads ". . . when you come together as a church," and 1 Corinthians 14:23 adds, "If therefore the whole church should assemble together." These verses are speaking directly to and about the assembly of Christians in the New Testament. There are few things more clearly taught than that Christians need to be together for the purpose of edification (1 Cor 14:3, 12, and 26). Where is the verse that connects all this with a formal worship? How do we know that "comes together" was a euphemism New Testament Christians use "to describe the gathering of Christians for worship"?

When Christians come together and edify one another, as God called us to do, He is worshiped through our obedience to Him, but where do we get the biblical right to call it THE WORSHIP? History and tradition say that it is, but the Bible nowhere does.

As mentioned before, in Matthew 18:20 when Jesus talks about "two or three" coming together in His name, He is not talking, even remotely, about the Christian assembly. He's still under the Old Law at the time He said it, and the subject was church discipline, not a formal worship. It sounds so traditional — it fits our presuppositions perfectly, but we have to take it completely out of context to use it. "The public worship of the church occurs only . . ." — and which Scriptures teach this? Worship can, but it doesn't have to be public, and it certainly doesn't have to have two or three. One act of compassion in the name of Jesus at any time is as much worship as a thousand people meeting in any facility on Sunday morning. Maybe more, if the thousand don't edify one another like they are supposed to.

Traditional thinking about worship is so ingrained in

our heads that we don't even realize it violates the Restoration plea and good logic. It violates the Restoration plea because we're not trying to be "simply and only New Testament Christians." We didn't get our doctrinal conclusions from Scripture, but rather the traditional practices of post-First Century religions. It is so strongly accepted that we don't see the inconsistency of speaking where the Bible doesn't speak. We actually become guilty of using reverse logic. It goes something like this:

— We call what we do in the assembly "worship."
— We look in the New Testament and see that they do what we do.
— Therefore, what they did must have been worship, and that settles it — the Christian assembly is THE worship.

If the Christian assembly was as major an event and so dominant in religious life for the New Testament Christians as it is for us today, and if we are so sure that they didn't just meet together but they met for THE worship, how could the entire New Testament record possibly have avoided referring to it as THE worship? How could something as important as going to Sunday worship have been completely left out?

Is it possible that as we strive to be just like they were in the New Testament, and we look back through the filters of the Restoration Movement, the Reformation, and centuries of Catholicism, that we have been influenced by those filters? Is it possible that the clutter of history prevents us from seeing the simplicity of the Christian assembly and the challenge to live lives of worship to God? Is it possible that the traditional view of worship was so strongly in place by the eighteenth century that men like Campbell and Stone never thought to question it? Do we think that their Restoration Movement was complete and total, or that they merely started something that sincere Christians will be working on when the Lord comes?

These are difficult and to some, troubling questions, but if they cause us to think as we open our hearts and our Bibles, they can present some exciting possibilities. After all, the truth sets us free. The most important thing for us is to make sure that we don't just dwell on what worship isn't, but what it is.

Before we turn our attention to what real worship is, can we be fairly sure that formal worship came from historical traditions instead of the Bible?

There's not space enough in this book to fully examine worship in religious history. There are plenty of books available for those who would like to do a deeper study (start with my bibliography). It is possible to trace our worship traditions back through the years to just after the first century. In short, it parallels the establishing of the Catholic church. Many of the traditions that came along immediately following the first century became institutionalized when Constantine declared Christianity the state religion. Catholicism formalized worship as a place and time which it called the Mass, making it an essential sacrament of the church. Through the years they established the priesthood, erected cathedrals, and created the papacy. In effect, Christianity returned to the temple worship of the Old Testament.

While the Reformation movement attempted to correct the abuses of Catholicism, it never questioned the place of worship in the life of believers. Two centuries later, the Restoration movement attempted to correct the errors of Protestantism, but it too did little to examine the traditional understanding of worship. It did call for the inclusion of all New Testament "acts of worship" like weekly communion for everyone, but there was continued traditional acceptance of Sunday being the day of worship. As I have pointed out before, it seems only natural that worship should go from the tabernacle, to the temple, to the cathedral, and finally to the church building.[14]

While formal-traditional worship can be easily traced back to the second and third centuries, it comes to a sudden stop at the book of Revelation. Religious historians can tell you when nearly every element of formalized worship began, from the sacramental-sanctuary mindset to the introduction of church furniture, such as pews, pulpits, communion tables, and special trays. We can follow the beginning of certain religious activities and see them become institutionalized, formalized, and canonized through time.

In James White's book *Protestant Worship*, he has a large section on "Frontier Worship" in which he shows where many of our traditions came from. These are

> worship practices that acquired their distinctive character-
> istics on the American frontier. These practices, in turn,
> influenced the worship of churches and sects that never
> came near the frontier but adopted what had become
> dominant characteristics of American Protestant worship.
> We can speak of denominations such as Southern Baptist,
> Disciples of Christ, and Churches of Christ as within the
> Frontier tradition.

He describes this tradition as being very pragmatic and evangelistic. Thus there was an emphasis on weekly communion, a specific order of worship, the use of invitations, and to facilitate traveling ministers, the addition of a Sunday evening worship. The popularity of the Frontier tradition was in part due to its ability to assist in making new converts. As White says, "Americans respect success, and here is a form of worship that has proven itself thoroughly successful in reaching the unchurched who happen to be present."[15] Of course, that was a day and time when "going to church" was popular, social, and the only game in town.

Much of what White discusses as "Frontier Worship" covers the period of history we refer to as the Restoration Movement. What White helps us see is that while there is a movement to "be simply and only New Testament Christians," there is a simultaneous Americanization of the Sunday morning (and now evening) worship service. At the very time some were trying to throw off Catholic and Protestant traditions, others were creating new ones, and calling them "part of the worship" or "essential to the worship."

Thus the American religious experience built on and enhanced the historical/traditional view of Sunday as THE day of worship. Everything about history supports that view; it's only when we go to the New Testament that we have a difficult time finding any support.

DISCUSSION QUESTIONS

1. Where did the idea come from that worship is what we do at the church building on Sunday morning?

2. What Scriptures are used to justify this view of worship?

3. Why is the assembly not THE worship?

4. How much of what we do in our assemblies actually comes from post-New Testament times?

5. Would you agree or disagree with the statement: "Much of our understanding of worship has historical roots but no biblical roots"?

CHAPTER 9
It *Is* in There Somewhere!

Worship is a life given in obedience to God. It's not a when or where proposition, but a what. It's what we are. You can't go to it or leave it, dress for it or from it, and you can't start it or stop it. It's not formal or informal, horizontal or vertical, and it's also not high or low, or contemporary or traditional. It doesn't open and close with a prayer, and it doesn't have a human leader or a special day. Worship is not corporate or private, and it isn't "five acts," and it's not so much what we do to God as what we do for (in the name of) God.

It is not my intent to rewrite *Spilt Grape Juice*, which deals extensively with defining worship, but I would like to more thoroughly expose what the Bible says on the subject as well as play the roll of an apologist for the aforementioned definition of worship.

The hard part is not the biblical exegesis, but rather removing the clutter of nineteen centuries of human presuppositions about worship. I know of no other doctrine where even the staunchest restorationist carries so many assumptions into the examination, and where there is such a cavalier attitude about applying Old Testament Scriptures to New Testament subjects. With that in mind, let's try to avoid both of those hindrances in our study. It's almost impossible, but try to forget everything you know about worship. Imagine your brain being a clean slate (or legal pad if you must be contemporary). Since Jesus said that all our notions about worship would have to change with the coming of the New Covenant, we won't even refer to it unless it's to point out a change or contrast. (See John 4:19-24.)

We must understand that words, especially religious words, have both denotations (explicit meanings as in the dictionary) and connotations (things suggested or associated with them). Connotations come from our experiences and memories, and they cause us to automatically have a mental picture, or feeling, about the word which may be dramatically different than its dictionary definition. This is one way that words change their meaning through the years and become archaic, or even change to completely different words. If you don't believe that's possible, ask your children what the word "bad" means.

Translators have a difficult task because they must not only interpret the original language, but they must find a word or phrase in our language that accurately gives the meaning of each word being translated. They are influenced by many things, not the least of which is their own connotation of words. We probably wouldn't have the word "baptism" today if it were not for the King James translators not wanting to translate the Greek word *baptizo* as immerse or bury. It was politically correct to just transliterate it into English and let some other translator worry about accuracy and the axe of the king.

How did the translators of the Bible know when to use

the word "worship" to best represent the Greek word or words used? Most of the time it was based on accepted and traditional practices and sometimes it was just a judgment call. That is why you will see some discrepancies between the different translations. When you add to that our connotations of worship, it becomes even more difficult to objectively examine what the New Testament really says about it.

The easiest way to approach the study of worship is to read every verse in the New Testament that uses the word "worship." Get a computer printout from one of the new Bible Study programs. It will only be four or five pages long. Then read them and make a list of every principle about worship that you discover. You'll be amazed at how brief the information is and how much we have openly filled in the blanks with our traditions.

After presenting just such a study of worship, Vine's *Expository Dictionary* declares, "The worship of God is nowhere defined in Scripture. A consideration of the above verbs shows that it is not confined to praise; broadly it may be regarded as the direct acknowledgment to God, of His nature, attributes, ways and claims, whether by the outgoing of the heart in praise and thanksgiving or by deed done in such acknowledgment."[16]

The most often translated word for worship in the New Testament is *proskuneo*. As mentioned before, it means to "make obeisance, do reverence to," and it comes from *pros*, meaning "towards" and *kuneo*, which means "to kiss."[17] It is used around 58 times in some 55 different verses. It is used in reference to homage paid to God, Christ, and man, and in Revelation it's done to the Dragon, the Beast, the image of the Beast, to demons, and to idols.

I read an article that strongly advocated *proskuneo* as the correct word for Christian worship today because it is used 58 times in the New Testament, while *latreuo* is only use five times. I guess that's interpretation by numbers, and I've never heard it used to justify any other doctrine. Still, we must recognize the widespread use of the word, but does it matter that over one-third of the occurrences are in Revelation and referring to false or incorrect worship and things that take place in heaven? Does it matter that over half of the uses are in the Gospels, before the church is established and the New Covenant is even in effect? Does it matter that of the seven times left when *proskuneo* is used it refers to idol worship (Acts 7:43), Jewish temple worship (Acts 8:27, 24:11), worship of man (Acts 10:25), worship of angels (Heb. 1:6), and Jacob in pre-Law days (Heb. 11:21)? The only other time it is used is in regard to the visitor to the assembly who sees a Christlike spirit in members and it causes him to fall "down on his face" and "worship God" (1 Cor. 14:25). There's nothing to indicate that he is even a Christian.

The point is that it's irrelevant whether *proskuneo* is used 58 times, or 1000 times. Not once is it used in connection with Christians and the Christian assembly! The most important usage of *proskuneo* is found in John 4:19-24, when Jesus tries to show that bowing down and doing obeisance is no longer a matter of time and place, but spirit and truth. The New Covenant took homage and obeisance to a higher level by expecting it to be internalized and total. Do we still bow down and do obeisance? Absolutely, but not in a sanctuary with man-made altars and idols, or during certain hours that are more holy than others!

We bow down and do obeisance in our hearts, and this translates to being submissive servants who carry out God's plan for us by being Christlike in every way we can. When that happens, God is praised, glorified, exalted, and worshiped, because He's been obeyed. This is the New Covenant relationship with God. It's the new challenge to live totally for Him.

In Romans 11, Paul was praising God for His mercy in offering the Gospel to both Jews and Gentiles. He declared,

"Oh, the depth of the riches both of the wisdom and knowledge of God! How unsearchable are His judgments and unfathomable His ways!" (v. 33) The last verse of the chapter says, "For from Him and through Him and to Him are all things. To Him be the glory forever. Amen" (v. 36) This message of how wonderful God is, is followed by a plea for us to give ourselves to Him completely. Paul said,

> I urge you therefore, brethren, by the mercies of God, to present your bodies a living and holy sacrifice, acceptable to God, which is your spiritual service of worship. (Rom 12:1).

Our new covenant relationship with God involves the giving of our lives to Him as living and holy sacrifices. We put ourselves on the altar of life and offer ourselves totally to Him, every day for as long as He lets us live. This is worship. This is the only worship in the new covenant that is acceptable and spiritual. Paul compares new covenant worship to the old covenant practice of sacrificing animals. It was a small sacrifice to make for the owner of the sheep or goat, but a total sacrifice for the animal. Of course, the animal had no choice in the matter. Now the follower of Christ is called on to choose to take the place of that dumb animal, and allow himself to become the offering to God. It's a living sacrifice, but one that involves dying to self in order that Christ might live through us.

The Greek word for worship in this verse is *latreuo*, which can be translated as either worship or service. This is why you will see it translated by some versions as service, some as worship, and some as "service of worship." Some argue that it must be translated as service, because it's not talking about worship and worship and service are two different things.

That is a classic defense of traditional thinking, but it has no foundation in Scripture. I don't believe it's an accident that Paul used *latreuo* in this passage. The very point he was trying to get us to understand is that worship and service are interchangeable, identical, and synonymous. We are worshiping creatures because we are servants, and to obey is to worship. Worship was never meant to be *a ministry of the church*, but rather *the lifestyle of each church member*.

Another interesting passage where *latreuo* is used is Hebrews 12:28-29:

> Therefore, since we receive a kingdom which cannot be shaken, let us show gratitude, by which we may offer to God an acceptable service with reverence and awe; for our God is a consuming fire.

As a result of being part of His kingdom, we must respond properly. We must show gratitude. Okay, we just have to say, "Thanks, God," and we've got that one covered, right? Wrong! This gratitude involves an offering or a sacrifice, and it must be acceptable to God. What is it? *Latreuo* – service or worship; the kind Paul described as "living." And isn't it interesting that this living offering is given with "reverence and awe?" The only time I ever heard folks talk about reverence and awe, they were talking about the acceptable demeanor in the Sunday worship. The biggest objection brethren gave for why we shouldn't stand and greet one another at the beginning of the assembly was that it destroyed the "reverent atmosphere." The same argument was made for why we shouldn't applaud after a baptism.

It's amazing to me that the only time in inspired writing that it talks about reverence, it's talking about a lifestyle attitude and has nothing to do with "a formal worship service." The point is clear and exciting: worship is a life given in gratitude to God! Is that saying the same thing as "a life given in obedience to God?" What do you think? Jesus said, "If you love Me, you will keep My commandments" (John 14:15).

One other passage really nails down this point beautifully. This passage spells out exactly what God is looking for from our "living sacrifice." Read this slowly:

> Through Him then, let us continually offer up a sacrifice of praise to God, that is, the fruit of lips that give thanks to His name. And do not neglect doing good and sharing; for with such sacrifices God is pleased (Heb 13:15-16).

Through whom do we offer a sacrifice? Jesus. How often do we offer this sacrifice? Continually. What is the sacrifice of praise to God? "..the fruit of lips that give thanks to His name." It's not just the praising, but "the fruit" or what the praising causes. What is a pleasing sacrifice to God? Doing good and sharing.

The kind of worship God wants is a living sacrifice that manifests itself through unselfishness and compassion. Every act of "doing good" and every act of "sharing" is a real, biblical act of worship.

Is the assembly worship? When we assemble are we being obedient to God? Hopefully we are, so it must be worship. When we meet together for fellowship, and strengthen and edify one another, it's worship because we are obeying God. It is worship because we are "doing good and sharing" not because we call it "the worship." There is nothing in the New Testament that says there is any other reason to call it worship, separate and apart from any other time when we might do good or share.

This is more than simply a matter of which Greek word best describes New Testament worship. This is about a consistent confirmation of God's desire for total conversion on our part. There is no place for segmenting our lives. We are either Christians all the way and all the time, or we're not Christians. Worship is a spiritual quality, and what spiritual qualities are there that God only wants us to have some of the time? These are all-inclusive concepts that we choose to live by. For example, to glorify God is to worship God. When do we glorify God? Paul said, "Whether, then, you eat or drink or whatever you do, do all to the glory of God" (1 Cor 10:31). It's obvious that we glorify God with our entire lives, or at least we should. Legalists may gripe and say, "Surely eating and drinking are too mundane and social to be worship to God!" But, does God want us to eat and drink, within healthy parameters of course? Sure He does, and just because it involves food doesn't mean we stop reflecting Jesus in our lives.

When I was in college and I shared this idea with one of my professors, he exploded and said, "You mean when I'm yelling and screaming at the football game that it's the same as singing hymns in church on Sunday morning?" He then waved off my idea with an implied message that it was too ludicrous to address any further. I would love to have been able to answer him. Is it less important to glorify God at a football game than it is at a "Sunday worship?" If what we are doing doesn't glorify God, maybe we shouldn't be doing it. It's a lot easier to look the part of a faithful churchgoer than it is to ask the tough questions like: "Would Jesus scream at referees? Can you visualize Jesus booing at a game?" Maybe there's a good reason why Satan wants us to think of worship as a Sunday-only activity.

The same argument for total-life-worship can be made about praise, thanksgiving, rejoicing, obedience, love, and a score of other life-enveloping spiritual concepts. Even the traditionalists will admit that worship must include being with Jesus, other Christians, and celebrating His sacrifice. That's exactly how John described the Christian life in 1 John 1:7. He said, ". . . if we walk in the light as He Himself is in the light, we have fellowship with one another, and the blood of Jesus His Son cleanses us from all sin." The presence of Jesus, fellowship with brethren, and forgiveness of sins, are all things "we walk in." Walk is a metaphor for living. We live in His light together every minute of every day. We assemble regularly to rejoice in that togetherness and not to pick up where we left off the week before.

DISCUSSION QUESTIONS

1. Why is it so difficult for us to be objective in our study of worship?

2. What does it mean to you that the word "worship" is never used in the New Testament in connection with the assembly?

3. Paul said that worship was a "living sacrifice." What does that mean to you?

4. If worship is our life, is the assembly worship?

5. Is worship a "walk" or a "visit?"

CHAPTER 10
The Language of Worship: Theology or Sociology?

The last several chapters that you just read are all part of number eight. Number eight of what, you ask? Thanks for asking! The eighth reason why the assembly is a battleground for Christians. It was just too big a reason to make it a subpoint. The preceding chapters simply make it clear that the assembly is a battleground because we don't understand the New Testament teaching about worship. Because of centuries of traditional thinking about worship, we have made the Sunday assembly the Top Banana instead of seeing it as just part of the bunch.

The assembly was never described as or intended to be The Worship of the church. It has been a basic assumption for so long that we have filled the silence of the Scriptures with a whole new vocabulary to justify our traditional preferences, and these words or redefined terms have become just as sacred as if they were given to us by God Himself.

Paul admonished Timothy to keep his flock focused on

God's will. He told him to "solemnly charge them in the presence of God not to wrangle about words, which is useless, and leads to the ruin of the hearers." Still, this must be tempered with the need to "Be diligent" as God's "workman who does not need to be ashamed, handling accurately the word of truth" (2 Tim 2:14-15). It's never just "wrangling about words" when one is attempting to determine God's truths. If new words, or words that have had their original definition completely changed, are presented as "the word of truth" when they are not, isn't that more than just a problem with semantics?

If you don't think that traditional thinking has changed biblical terminology, just ask any Christian where they go on Sunday morning. More than likely you will get one of three answers: "I go to church," "I go to worship," or "I go to services." Of course there are a multitude of combinations, like church services, worship services, or church worship services. We all use these terms to describe what we attend on Sunday morning. Now, find any of these words being used that way in the Bible. A first century Christian would not have even known what we were talking about if we used these terms this way in their presence.

Someone says, "It's not a big deal, right? We all know what we are talking about when we use these terms this way, and besides, it's just too difficult to change a millennium of tradition." I have said these things too, but I have a difficult time dealing with certain questions like:

Do we change "the truth" by using these words in an unbiblical way?

Are we ready to stop saying that we "call Bible things by Bible names?"

Do we really want the assembly to stop being a battleground?

Maybe it is a big deal. Maybe it's time to recognize that we have interpreted the New Testament with traditional presuppositions that are wrong. The truthfulness of a doctrine is not determined by its longevity, but by its biblical foundation. You cannot biblically justify or defend the traditional understanding of the assembly as THE church, THE worship, or THE services. Try it! Get out your concordance and Bible dictionary, and prove it to yourself. Don't use a commentary, however, because the writer will start out with preconceived assumptions about those terms.

In writing to the brethren in Corinth, Paul had several things to say about their assemblies. He referred to their assembly as "when you come together as a church," and when "the whole church should assemble together" (1 Cor 11:18; 14:23). They were the church before and after they came together, but they were to assemble as a group of people who the Lord had added to the church. Not only do we superimpose our traditional assumptions on this record by calling their assembly THE worship, but we have created an array of words to better describe it. Their togetherness, as well as our own, is regularly referred to as THE FORMAL WORSHIP, or THE CORPORATE WORSHIP, or even THE PUBLIC WORSHIP. The terms "formal," "corporate," and "public" may have originally been used as adjectives, but they have been pronouns for a long time now, and they're still not found in the Bible.

Where did the idea of a formal worship come from? It didn't come from the New Testament. Even if you want to insist that the Sunday assembly is The Worship, where is the biblical precedent for calling it formal? The truth is, if we consider our togetherness a formal worship service, it's because we want it and not because God expects it. The very act of calling it formal elevates the assembly to a religious rite that is completely man-made, man centered, and authorized only by tradition.

Why is Sunday morning more formal than Sunday evening, or even Wednesday evening? What is it that makes it THE formal worship? Is it the Lord's Supper?

Don't you have a make-up session on Sunday evening for those "providentially hindered?" What's the difference between a formal worship and a devotional? That should be easy since we can't use the Bible to define either one! Yet somehow we know the difference. I was rebuked by an elder once for saying that our Sunday evening assembly was going to be a devotional. He told me that it was offensive to some members for me to refer to it as a devotional, because it diminished the importance of what we were going to do and emphasized that it would be "less formal." I thought that was understood! That's why I don't have to wear a tie on Sunday evening, while on Sunday morning there are folks who can't hear the sermon if they don't see a coat and tie on the preacher.

Also, by putting the word "formal" before worship, we create a convenient religious dichotomy for our lives. By bracketing the formal worship between two other man-made rituals, the opening and closing prayer, we are then free to do things at other times that we believe can't be done in the formal assembly. For those who believe that Christians can only sing spiritual songs without instrumental music, they are free to go home and sing hymns with their piano all they want, because it's not the formal assembly. And of course, women can talk all they want before and after those magical opening and closing prayers, because being silent in the church is referring to the formal assembly. Five minutes before that opening prayer, the same women in the same building, sitting in the same seats, could comment, share, and edify others, simply because it was called "a Bible class," and everyone knows that's not the same as the formal worship. There is some sense of consistency in this; neither Bible classes nor formal worship are found in the New Testament, so we can make up the rules as we go.

In the Bible God simply says that He wants Christians to come together in a spirit of love to build one another up.

The assembly is shared encouragement! It's strength through numbers! It's a time of celebrating our mutual gift of grace and the One who paid the price for it. Satan must get a full belly laugh every time a Christian refers to the assembly of saints as "the formal worship." He loves it when we complicate things, emphasize the externals, and turn an unselfish act into a self-righteous work.

Many people have concluded that worship is something we can do anytime and anywhere, and it can't be qualified by the number of participants. They believe that whether it's one, ten, or a thousand worshiping, it's worship in each situation. They still need a way to distinguish the "whole church" or the more "formal worship" from the partial church worship, so they use the designation "corporate" or "public" worship.

"Corporate" is a nonbiblical term that is used for merely practical reasons. It is used as a contrast to smaller group assemblies, and generally just means the church all together. It's sort of a technical word used to clarify what is being discussed. If the whole congregation attends, could you have a corporate funeral, or a corporate wedding? (Just kidding!)

"Public," like the word "corporate," is used as a contrast with "private." Both of these terms are used within the framework of worship being something you do, something you go to and leave. Not only is that inaccurate, but the idea of being public about any spiritual activity is something Jesus personally discouraged. I believe that His comments in the Sermon on the Mount about prayer, fasting, and giving are further support for the changes in our relationship with God that the New Covenant would usher in.

Most of the religious rituals of the Old Covenant were done in public, usually during feasts or with multitudes at the temple. Some of the Jews, in particular the Pharisees, became especially showy about their faithfulness to the law. They were doing things publicly, to be seen by men.

Jesus said to do these things in private, even secretly. These spiritual acts were to be so private that He said, "do not let your left hand know what your right hand is doing." (See Matt 6:1-7.).

Does that mean that our assemblies cannot be public? Not necessarily, but it is difficult to see the New Testament Christians who met in private homes thinking of their togetherness as public. Certainly those later Christians who feared for their lives as they hid in the catacombs didn't think of the assembly as being public. Then again, just because the front doors on our church building are unlocked, it doesn't mean we're being public. If we had our assembly out on the lawn or in the parking lot, that would be public, but then we probably couldn't call it "the formal worship," especially if we took our ties off. And, if it's not formal that means that we can . . . . oh well, that's another story.

WORDS, WORDS, AND MORE WORDS!

Webster says that semantics is "the branch of linguistics concerned with the nature, structure, and, especially, the development and changes, of the meanings of words."[18] I have always been fascinated by words. It is exciting to follow the root word back to its origins and see how a single word can change so many times throughout the centuries.

Back in the Dark Ages, when I took Greek in college, the most thrilling moments I had in class were the times I knew what a Greek word meant because it clearly was the root word of an English word. A word like *kardia* would appear on our vocabulary list, and I could immediately tell that it was the Greek word for heart. It was obviously the root word for cardiac, cardiogram, and cardiology. And the Greek word *grapho* was the word for write, and is clearly the root word for graphic, graphic art, and graphology (the study of handwriting). These words are centuries old, but just a few decades ago, science and technology put them together to create a new word, cardiograph. It's not difficult to figure out what that means, is it? It's literally an instrument that gives a record of the heart. Isn't that neat?

I love words. It's incredible what the appropriately constructed group of words can accomplish. On top of that, there is nothing static about words. They are constantly changing, evolving, and carrying different connotations for each person. I have an outline for a future book I want to write some day about preaching and the work of the preacher. I plan to entitle it *Whacking Elephants*. I like the weird title because it is an evolved expression that represents the constantly changing nature of preaching. Every preacher or public speaker has heard of, and maybe even received, the old compliment, "You waxed eloquent today, Preacher." In college we all made fun of that archaic flattery by saying, "You waxed an elephant today." For years that was a standard joke my wife and I used to describe my preaching for that particular day. One day, after saying that in the presence of my children, one of my daughters asked, with great concern, "Daddy, why would you want to whack an elephant?"

Guess what? Now when I need to tell my family that I am pleased with how I did that day, I simply say, "Boy I really whacked an elephant today." Words change and sometimes they are completely replaced by new words — that's life!

Much of our worship vocabulary doesn't come from the Bible. That's not necessarily wrong or bad. It merely confirms that we constantly introduce new terms to help us better communicate. The problem with religious words is that they may reflect, endorse, and propagate error by giving credibility to something not found in Scripture. The problem can be further compounded by people believing the new word to be as much of a spiritual absolute as Scripture itself.

This is most easily seen in the discussion (battles) about expediencies. For example, have you found songbooks in your Bible yet? Songbooks or hymnals are totally a matter of expediency, and yet brethren are willing to fight-to-the-death over which book is not best, but right; which color cover is acceptable, and whether or not putting songs on an overhead projector is scriptural. Is this not a natural result of centuries of promoting a formal worship? The more people focus on a single time and place to do their "worship thing" the more the expression is true that "the devil is in the details."

To enhance, and finally protect, our worship time, we codify expediencies and the language used to describe them, forgetting that these things didn't come from the Word of God. Please let me emphasize again that there is nothing in themselves wrong with these terms or phrases. The problem is the lack of biblical knowledge that causes people to place their traditions over the Truth. I've mentioned the songbook, but an even better example is the song leader.

When you have a formal worship, it just makes sense to have formal songbooks and an official song leader to make sure that everything is done "decently and in order." This is another logical conclusion based on erroneous assumptions. In most assemblies the song leader is more central to what happens than the preacher. How is it that there is no record of any song leader in the New Testament? They sang, and someone had to start it, but who? Is it wrong to have a song leader? Of course not, but how many members realize that it is just a man-made expediency and not a scriptural requirement? If you don't think there are folks in your congregation who don't know the difference, let a group of three or four men lead singing next Sunday and then listen to the comments that people have. They won't argue the effectiveness of it, but they will let you know quickly that it's wrong, unbiblical, and the work of the devil. They don't seem to know that the Scripture authorizing one song leader also authorizes three or four — or fifty.

The language of formal worship is constantly changing. The New Testament doesn't say a thing about invitation songs, congregational meditation, pastoral counseling, or Hug Happenings to close out the formal worship. There's nothing wrong with any of these things, but we just need to remember that they came from our belief in the existence of a formal worship time and not from the Word. Whether we decide to have a song leader or a praise team, whether we have an MC or a worship leader, whether we have an opening prayer, an intercessory prayer, or a Call to Worship, it's okay, but they are all creations of man to support our formal worship. The only "call to worship" I can infer from New Testament Scripture is the call to live for Jesus.

Someone says, "You're just arguing about semantics." Absolutely, just like we have always done because of our commitment to "speak where the Bible speaks." Have you ever argued about the difference between sprinkling and immersion? Do you feel comfortable calling communion the "eucharist?" I don't have the word "Reverend" in front of my name on my business cards, and I don't like to think of myself as clergy and my brethren laity.

How do we decide on the vocabulary we use? You know the answer to that, it's the Word of God. Sometimes words are just flat scripturally wrong, but other times they are just inaccurate or given more credence than they deserve. Many of our worship terms have come from our traditional understanding of worship as something we do at a specific place and time, and that is an unbiblical starting point. They are not necessarily wrong; they just reinforce that incorrect presupposition.

This is not a call for widespread repentance or for the wholesale rejection of these terms. I am making this point to simply show how pervasive our traditional worship assumptions are and how they affect every element of our assembly. It's not just our assembly either.

We like to say that "the church" is not brick and mortar, but folks still think of the church building, specifically the auditorium, as the sanctuary, and refer to it as "the House of God." Look at your church budget. How much money is earmarked for "Worship?" The formal worship requires thousands of dollars for furniture, books, utilities, mortgages, worship leaders, and preachers, whose primary job is presenting a "knock'em out" sermon so we can attract and keep plenty of people in our "primary worship." Compare this to the Christian assemblies in the New Testament, which were simple, homemade get-togethers, with only two budget items: mission and benevolence.

Again, I am not proposing that all those "worship" things are wrong. They are, however, expediencies developed to support "the formal worship" of the church. In fact, the single most important element in judging faithfulness, and hence, choosing church leaders, is attendance to "worship." Jesus judged faithfulness by examining compassion. Do we feed the hungry, clothe the naked, visit the sick and imprisoned? Those who "inherit the kingdom prepared" for them are those who showed compassion "even to the least of them," not those who met with the rest of us. (See Matt 25:31-46.) Hopefully these are not mutually exclusive spiritual qualities, but it does illustrate how "formal worship" thinking changes how we define terms.

Not only is it used to judge faithfulness, but it is used as the standard by which we judge doctrinal soundness too. There was a time when a liberal was someone who rejected the virgin birth of Christ, the inspiration of the Bible, or the doctrine of the Trinity. Who are the liberals today? Anyone who is more progressive in their worship than I am! Scripture doesn't count anymore, or so it seems. The liberals aren't the folks who think James doesn't belong in the Bible, but rather those brethren who sing during the passing of the communion, have praise teams, or do a dramatic skit during "THE worship" to make a spiritual point.

Who are the conservatives now? If I like that label, it's me. If I think it's derogatory, a conservative then becomes anyone who thinks it's wrong to be as progressive as I am in "THE worship" — you know, those narrow-minded brethren who still have to have two songs and a prayer, in that order — no matter what. They're the "old fogies" who only sing four-hundred-year-old hymns, insist on the sermon before (or after) the communion, and act like "THE worship" is a funeral. "They're just not as enlightened as we are or as free in Christ."

Isn't it amazing how our preferences about "the formal worship" give us the right to judge and even malign those who don't agree with us? What's sad is that we are arguing, labeling, and being unkind about something that's not even in the Bible. Maybe that's why so many become so un-Christlike so quickly as we fight on this battleground.

DISCUSSION QUESTIONS

1. Why do we call going to the assembly going to church, worship, or services?

2. Where did the concept of a formal worship come from?

3. What are some of the practical reasons why we separate our time together into formal and informal worship?

4. What are some words that we regularly use in the assembly that are purely expediencies and not from the Bible?

5. When do we need to become concerned about semantics?

135

CHAPTER 11
Imprisoned Truths

By the time the sun was up that morning on March 6, 1836, the battle for the Alamo was virtually over. It took longer to show the 1960 movie version, which was produced, directed, and starred John Wayne, than it did to fight the actual battle. As the smoke began to clear and the shooting and screaming stopped, seven defenders of the Alamo were captured alive and taken to Santa Anna. When he saw the seven, he quickly ordered their execution. They were immediately hacked and bayoneted to death by the soldiers surrounding them. One of the seven men was Davy Crockett.

While there are some who dispute the claim that Crockett was one of those seven men, there seems to be adequate evidence that it is true. There are plenty of historical facts that have much less evidence than this does, but because of the tremendous emotional feelings about the Alamo and the heroes who died there, many just simply refuse to believe it. Especially since the mid 1950s, when Fess Parker portrayed a rifle-swinging Davy Crockett who went down fighting, to suggest that he surrendered is inconceivable. An eyewitness identified Crockett as one of the seven, but tradition and myth-driven emotionalism says it couldn't have been him. So for many, the truth is imprisoned and they'd just as soon it stay that way.

The New Covenant worship is not something done one hour on Sunday. Christian worship is a life given in obedience to God. We have eyewitnesses who identified it for us, but centuries of tradition speak louder than inspired writers, and the truth stays imprisoned. Not only is the New Testament concept of worship imprisoned by tradition, but many spiritual words and concepts are imprisoned or at least restricted by it too. Not in the sense that they are locked away and forgotten, but in the sense that they are severely limited by the traditional narrow definition of worship.

For example, when, where, and how do we praise God? Even though we know better, we still tend to think of it as something we do "at church on Sunday." Many folks even define worship as "going to church and praising God." Where do we find that idea in the New Testament? It sounds right — because that is what we've always been told, but is that how the early Christians understood praise?

Praise means to commend or express the worthiness of something or someone. To praise God is to pay homage, extol, give thanks, sing, glorify, and, in general, speak highly of Him. Hopefully this is done when we assemble together, but is that the when, where, and how described in the New Testament? Where did we get the idea that praising God was only or even primarily a Sunday event? Was it because that is usually the only time we sing, and singing is described as praising God? Paul and Silas "were praying and singing hymns of praise to God" at about midnight while in prison with their feet locked up in stocks (Acts 16:25). I wonder what night of the week it was? It wasn't Sunday because the day before was clearly not the Sabbath.

Which of these two illustrations best exemplify the New Testament doctrine of praise? It's Sunday morning and seven hundred Christians are solemnly singing "Praise God from whom all blessings flow." At the same time, a deacon is missing the whole thing because a needy family walked into the office just as "THE worship" was starting, and now he is taking them to the church pantry to get them some food. Which one is praising God? Which is doing the most important thing? Which one is worshiping God? Suppose the Lord returned at that very instant and that deacon was not in attendance?

Both of these illustrations can and should be praising God, but it's possible that neither one is – if the heart of each participant is not right with God. God is praised by our obedience to Him, not just because we raise our voices and hands heavenward and say, "Praise the Lord."

The Psalmist said in Psalm 19:1, "The heavens are telling of the glory of God; and their expanse is declaring the work of His hands." In Psalm 8 he said, "O Lord, our Lord, how majestic is Thy name in all the earth, who hast displayed Thy splendor above the heavens! . . . When I consider Thy heavens, the work of Thy fingers, the moon and the stars, which Thou hast ordained; what is man, that Thou dost take thought of him?" (vv. 1,3,4) These and scores of other passages tell us that all of creation praises God. God is praised because what He created functions as it was created to function, not because the sun, moon, and stars shout, "Isn't God great!" The only created thing that doesn't function like God intended for it to function is man, and when man does what he should, God is praised. Every time!

Paul said, "we who were the first to hope in Christ

should be to the praise of His glory. In Him, you also, after listening to the message of truth, the gospel of your salvation—having also believed, you were sealed in Him with the Holy Spirit of promise, who is given as a pledge of our inheritance, with a view to the redemption of God's own possession, to the praise of His glory" (Eph 1:12-14).

Even though this is one of Paul's compound-complex sentences, it is still easy to understand. Paul said that when we became Christians God gave us His Spirit as a pledge of His plan to redeem us, and as His possession we ARE "to the praise of His glory." Praise is what we are and not just what we do. This is a powerful and sublime spiritual concept that has been virtually taken away by the insistence on traditional, formal worship. As long as you have to go somewhere to a special place and time to praise God, you won't feel the need to do it the other 167 hours of the week.

Again, the New Testament says nothing about going to God's house, on His day, to do anything FOR HIM. Yet we all grew up hearing, "Going to church is the least I can do for God after all He has done for me." Or maybe you heard, "We must dress up for church because it's the least we can do for God. It's His house and we must wear our best for Him." Thus it shouldn't be surprising that praise became something we do FOR God.

Satan loves it when we develop a small God who lives at the church building, or have a God who sits in judgment of our attire as we come into His presence on Sunday morning. He loves it when we teach and believe that God can be paid back simply by our attendance at church or because we have sent plenty of praises His way. Is our God a giant ego in the sky sucking up all the compliments and praises we can send His way on Sunday morning? Brethren, beware of the temptation of believing that God needs anything from us. Our God "does not dwell in temples made with hands; neither is He served by human hands, as though He needed anything, since He Himself gives to all life and breath and all things" (Acts 17:24-25). He does not need our praises. We need to praise Him, and we do that with every act of obedience to Him and even with every breath we take if we are "a living sacrifice" for Him.

Hopefully you have noticed that my definition of praise sounds a lot like the definition I've offered for worship. That is because they are nearly the same in the New Testament. Worship is praising God. Where one goes the other goes. So how and why did we ever limit praising God to something that is done for one hour on Sunday morning? Just answer the question, what do most people think worship is?

For all practical purposes, worship and praise are synonymous words in the New Testament when applied to what the child of God is and does. Another synonym of both these terms is glory or glorify. To glorify is to magnify, extol, praise, or ascribe honor to someone.[19] When we worship, praise, and glorify God, we are exalting Him. This means that we are reflecting positively on Him and showing His preeminence in our lives.

When my children do things that reflect positively on me as their father, I have, in a sense, been glorified by them. They reflect love, respect, appreciation, commendation, and commitment on me and about me to others. That's why I may gladly shout, "That's my girl" or "That's my boy" when they do something in public that I am especially proud of.

We glorify (praise and worship) God every time we reflect positively on Him. It may be an act of obedience, like feeding the hungry, or "admonishing one another in song," or it might simply be His spirit shining through in my attitude and the way I treat others. Any manifestation of a Christlike spirit is glorifying God. That is why Paul could say, "Whether, then, you eat or drink or whatever you do, do all to the glory of God" (1 Cor 10:31). It was not the eating and drinking that was glorifying God, but the Christlike spirit of unselfishness and consideration that reflected positively on God.

In spite of that, we still hear people say, "The purpose of the Sunday morning worship is to glorify God." Again, that sounds wonderful, even spiritual, but can it be proven with Scripture? It is so profound and so widely accepted there must be a verse in the New Testament somewhere that clearly supports that truth – isn't there? It's in church bulletins, church mission statements, and church policies so it must be in the Word – right?

Break out your concordance and check. Most concordances will have several pages listing hundreds of passages where glory, glorify, or some form of the word is used in the Bible. You can cut your search considerably by checking only the New Testament passages. While you're at it, just for fun, every place you see the word "glorify" being used in reference to God, replace it with the word "worship" or "praise" and see if it changes the meaning at all. (You'll find they are virtually interchangeable.)

If you don't want to "let your fingers do the walking" through the hallowed pages, you can take my word for it; there is no verse in the New Testament that says, "Sunday morning worship is to glorify God." The Scriptures never put the words "worship" or "glorify" with Sunday morning. That doesn't mean it's not supposed to happen, but it does mean that worshiping and glorifying God are much more than what our traditional practices have been. The Scriptures do say that when we get together everything is to be done for "edification." When we do that, we are being obedient to God and He is glorified, praised, and worshiped. The same is true for the "cup of water given in" His name – wherever and whenever it happens.

Again, the main reason for dwelling on this is to show how the assumption that worship is a formal Sunday morning activity has affected every element of our faith, doctrine, religious vocabulary, and our entire approach to interpreting Scripture. Am I "straining at a gnat?" I don't think so. Our goal is to be guided by Scripture, not to guide Scripture by our traditions.

Too much of our spiritual experience is centered around the assembly. Nearly every major element of what it means to live for Jesus is defined by "THE worship" hour. For instance, how much of our responsibility in the areas of service and sacrifice are defined almost completely by "church" attendance? The very act of attending is seen by many as their service to God — "It's the least we can do for Him." We even call it "THE services." The sum total of service for many is just being there, or if you are a REAL servant, you serve communion, lead singing, or offer a public prayer. It gave us a sense of motivation when we didn't really feel like it, but we got out of bed, dressed in our best for God, fought the ice, sleet, and snow to be at church, just to serve God. That is when it's not only an act of service, but of sacrifice. The crowning touch of which is each one sacrificing "as he may prosper" when the tray is passed, and fulfilling that task for another week.

This is not an indictment on the motivation of Christians around the world. Brethren are simply doing what they've been taught and what has been practiced for centuries. Preachers have raked members over the coals for being Sunday-only Christians, but our traditional approach to worship encourages it.

Not too long ago an older brother complained to me that he was embarrassed to bring his neighbors to worship because I didn't offer the whole plan of salvation in my invitation, which we all know every sermon must have. Brethren still see "THE worship" as the church's primary evangelistic thrust. I suspect the real reason many want to hear "THE PLAN" after every sermon is that it reenforces doctrinal orthodoxy, not because of all the unchurched visitors who have wandered into our building. Even then, the sum total of many congregations' outreach program is encouraging members to invite others to the Sunday morning worship. It is our evangelism ministry.

I guess that's all right, because the same passages that tell us that Sunday morning is THE time of worship also tell us to "let all things be done to" evangelize — right? One of those New Testament examples of the assembly surely has the Gospel plan of salvation being offered to non-Christians — right? Or is this perhaps another continuation of America's Frontier religious experience, with camp meetings, invitations, and itinerant preachers?

I am constantly amazed at the people who call me to tell me that their son or daughter has decided to become a Christian — Sunday after next, when their grandparents can be here. These are people who believe adamantly, without compromise, that everyone who wants to be a child of God must do as Peter commanded in Acts 2:38, "Repent, and let each of you be baptized in the name of Jesus Christ for the forgiveness of your sins; and you shall receive the gift of the Holy Spirit." In the same book of the Bible, when people decided to "put on Christ in baptism" they "ordered the chariot to stop; and they both went down into the water . . . and he baptized him" (the Ethiopian eunuch, Acts 8:25-40). In the case of Paul's conversion, he was told, "Why do you delay? Arise and be baptized, and wash away your sins" (Acts 22:16). Then there is the Philippian jailor, who wanted to be saved, "and immediately he was baptized" (Acts 16:31-34).

How can folks with such strong beliefs about following the New Testament pattern put off the baptizing of their children, when that is what they want? They feel the need to wait for the official Sunday morning worship. In fact, many parents even insist that their child "walk the aisle" and "make the good confession" in front of the whole congregation on Sunday morning. It's a sign of commitment to them and it's "the way we've always done it." While I appreciate anyone wanting a conversion to be a family affair for both spiritual and physical families, when someone realizes they are lost they need to be "buried with Christ" as soon as possible. Being covered by the cleansing blood of Jesus is more important than meeting with the Body of Christ even if we call it "THE worship."

Has the traditional view of worship affected how we think about conversions? Obviously it has, at least to many people. It is difficult for it not to affect it in view of the pre-eminence we give it, making it the focus of our religion and insisting that there is a special presence of God there too! Why would you be baptized at any other time?

What makes my heart ache is to think of all the people, young and old, who are not Christians today because they don't want to respond, confess, and be baptized in front of hundreds of people in the formal worship.

ENCOUNTERING GOD

We preacher-types get a kick out of saying, "Yeah, I like church work. It's the people that I don't like." That's a joke! We like to say it to humorously remind ourselves that we really are in the people business. It's amazing that any servant could possibly think otherwise. The church is people. It's the Body of Christ, and only He decides who is in or out. He is also the only One who we must listen to when it comes to how He is to be worshiped.

One of the most commonly used phrases to define worship or describe the purpose of worship is that it's an "encounter with God." Who can argue with that? It sounds so personal, so meaningful, and so spiritual, that one would be labeled heretical to dare question it. I agree with it. I have no problem declaring that worship is an encounter with God. But (you knew that was coming didn't you?) if what is meant by worship is the Christian assembly, I would have to strongly disagree. Why? There simply isn't any Scripture to back it up. This is another case of developing a vocabulary to support our traditions.

Those who would vociferously deny that the church building is "The House of God" have no problem with teaching that there is a special presence of God in the assembly. It's not in the Bible, so it must be a doctrine of man. It does provide justification for the importance of the assembly, and it helps support a formalism in the assembly with all the accompanying reverence and solemnity we traditionally feel must be present, but it's just not found in Scripture. That's true whether one wants to promote traditional styles or whether one wants an emotional experience which is enhanced by a special feeling that He is there.

Using the New Testament as your guide, how does one encounter God? We have been very adamant in rebuking the charismatic for believing in a special presence of God in convicting and converting alien sinners. He doesn't create saving faith by whispering in someone's ear or hitting them with a bolt of lightning. It has, is, and always will be true, that "faith comes by hearing, and hearing by the word of Christ" (Rom 10:17). Acceptable and obedient faith must be based on the Truth of God, and as a result of that obedience we receive the saving grace of God. "For by grace you have been saved through faith; and that not of yourselves, it is the gift of God," said Paul, and there is still only one place that faith comes from — the Word (Eph 2:8). We encounter God in the Bible.

Once we become children of God, He is in us and we are in Him. Our very bodies become His temple, and "in Him we live, and move, and have our very being." What is prayer for the Christian if it is not a personal encounter with God? Can we do that together, with others? Sure, but that is true anywhere, anytime, and for any reason.

A Sunday morning sermon may cause a person to be

confronted by God, but can't that happen anywhere and anytime too? In fact, we can be confronted with the reality of God anytime we stop and recognize His handiwork. I saw God when I watched our children being born. I saw God in the star-packed sky of Alaska. I see God in the beauties of nature every time I go hunting. Paul said:

> For since the creation of the world His invisible attributes, His eternal power and divine nature, have been clearly seen, being understood through what has been made . . . (Rom 1:20).

So there it is, forget going to church on Sunday to encounter God. Just take a hike in the country instead — NOT!

Before you tell me to "take a hike" let me tell you why you need to meet with your brethren on Sunday. When you meet with your church family on Sunday, there may not be a special presence of God, but there is a special gathering of godly people. Remember, that is true any time God's people get together, because He is the God of our lives and He goes wherever our hearts go.

The problem is that we keep telling folks that we worship to encounter God and they go away feeling like He forsook the assembly. We imply that He is present, separate and apart from all the others there, and are surprised that people's expectations are not met. Why else would we structure our assemblies to be quiet and meditative with little or no interaction, so that we don't "destroy the reverent atmosphere" we believe necessary? After all, isn't it directed towards Him and aren't we worshiping Him?

God is in our assembly because God is in us. Where in Scripture do you find anything about doing something for God separate and apart from what we do for others in His name? What we do for God is keep His commandments, but what are His commandments? John said, "And this is His commandment, that we believe in the name of His Son Jesus Christ, and love one another, just as He commanded us" (1 John 3:23). That is what He has always wanted from us. In fact, John is very emphatic about how we love God. The only way to know that you love God, are born of God, and have Him abiding in you is to love one another. (See 1 John 4:7-21.).

You want to see God in your assembly? Look in the right places. Listen to John:

> No one has beheld God at any time; if we love one another, God abides in us, and His love is perfected in us (1 John 4:12).

You will not see God in your assembly separate and apart from seeing Him in godly people. The absolute best way to worship God is to love one another. It doesn't happen any other way. How can we continue to let people believe that they can come into a church building on Sunday morning, sing a few songs, pray, commune quietly by themselves, listen to a sermon, leave, never having said more than two words to another person, and feel like they have worshiped God? Satan must laugh until his stomach hurts to see so many people believe that they "encountered God" when all they really did was follow a tradition of man.

How do you love God separate and apart from loving others? How do you serve God separate and apart from serving others? Jesus said that the way to serve Him was to serve "the least of these my brethren," those who needed food, clothing, caring, and visiting. We encounter Jesus, and God, in the day-to-day acts of compassion that we see in others, and ourselves.

Our life is given to worshiping God. Worship is an encounter with God. Our life, therefore, is an encounter with God.

DISCUSSION QUESTIONS

1. When, where, and how do we praise God?

2. Does it change your thinking about the words "praise" and "worship" to find out that they are synonymous?

3. When and how do we glorify God?

4. How can eating and drinking glorify God? (1 Cor 10:31)

5. Would it be wrong or a sin not to "offer the invitation" at the end of the Sunday morning sermon? Why or why not?

6. How do we encounter God in the assembly?

SECTION FOUR
Radical Worship

CHAPTER 12
The Ultimate Change Agent

I teach the Senior Bible class at a Christian school. I am constantly amazed with how much has changed since I was their age. They all carry book bags now! When I was in school only the nerds carried book bags, and most of them quit doing it after a few times of being made fun of. Today the guys button the top button on their shirts, which was a definite "no-no," and what's even stranger, they wear white socks with loafers. Again, only the socially inept did such things in the "good old days." The boys like to have the hair on the sides of their head shaved off, making it look like they got their hair cuts from a carpenter. When I was in school, we wanted our hair to look like the Beach Boys or the Beatles, and we had running battles with the administration about the definition of what was too long. I still remember the time two "old men" at church offered to pay for my haircut and toss in two dollars each if I'd just accept it. I think my hair was touching my eyebrows and my ears, and of course that made me nearly a Hippie. I guess they couldn't understand why we weren't like they were when they were in school. Imagine that!

Each generation has to define itself and develop its own identity. That is one of the many reasons why things are constantly changing, and why many will continually resent it and resist it. Nowhere is the resentment and resistance to change more prevalent than in religion.

To reduce the amount of resistance and resentment to change that can crop up when something different is done, we've devised several different forms of concealment. One of the truisms of church work is — it's not what you do, it's what you call it. To some folks, a solo in the assembly is unacceptable, but a soprano lead is traditionally okay. Some say it's wrong to have a choir, but a song sung by all the children down front before they're dismissed to Children's Worship is "being inclusive." Women can pass communion trays, just don't try to serve it. A preacher can "role play" as part of a sermon, just don't call it drama. Clergy robes are anathema, but the required coat and tie are just "appropriate."

Sometimes we play word games. The names may stay the same, but the changing still happens. If, however, you emphasize change, then you get labeled a "Change Agent." This has become a derogatory name for anyone who suggests that we have the right, and even the duty, to do things a little differently than the way we've done them in the past. They can't be called "liberal" because they only seek change in areas of expediency and not fundamental doctrine. So these man-made names are used to create the impression of unsoundness and having "ulterior motives," giving the impression that to suggest changes in tradition is tantamount to the work of the Devil.

The irony is that those who are labeled as Change Agents are usually motivated by a deep love for God's Word and a strong commitment to the Restoration plea.

They simply claim the right to be relevant, but to many that is the same as being radical. The true sad irony is that every congregation in the world wants to grow, but many don't want to change in order to make it happen. They hire a preacher and charge him with the task of creating growth, then slap his hand for trying to change anything from the way it has always been done.

Many church folks live by one simple creed: change is bad while traditions are good. And, to be fair, there are some who live by the opposite creed: traditions are bad while change is good. Like many things, neither perspective is true. Change and tradition are neither good nor bad, what matters is whether or not they are used to the glory of God.

Any change or tradition that is instituted or maintained at the expense of a spiritual principle is bad. A tradition that is elevated to law is wrong — period. At the same time, a change that ignores the spirit of Christ is wrong — period. The objective is to carry out the will of God, which means growing spiritually and bearing fruit, but when defending the "old ways" or promoting the "new ideas" becomes more important, we're totally wrong — exclamation point!

With that point firmly made, take a stab at answering the following question: Was Jesus a Traditionalist or a Change Agent? If we feel uncomfortable labeling Jesus, maybe we should feel the same way about labeling His disciples. Nevertheless, I think we all know which Jesus was; He was the ultimate Change Agent.

From His baptism by the reluctant John to His ascension He was changing preconceived notions, traditional thinking, and religious myopia. He was the epitome of change. He changed addresses from heaven to earth. He changed from being God and "became flesh and dwelt among us." He "grew in wisdom and stature, and in favor with God and man" (Luke 2:52). Growth is change, and He changed intellectually, physically, spiritually, and socially. It shouldn't be surprising that He changed others the same way.

How many of those who met and talked with Jesus grew intellectually? The teachers and rabbis in the temple when He was twelve were amazed by His wisdom. Nicodemus came to Jesus at night and asked Him some tough questions, and he got some thought-provoking answers in return. (See John 3:1-21.) What about the lawyers, teachers, and politicians who were shaken by His insights?

Jesus changed people physically too. Withered arms and legs started working, eyes were opened, diseased bodies were cleansed, and dead flesh came to life. He once made a whip and changed the changers. Another time He changed a sack lunch into a feast for thousands, and at another time He turned water into wine. He even changed the weather, the laws of gravity, and the finality of the grave.

In a theocracy like Israel, it's difficult to separate the social from the spiritual. That was really part of the problem. They had elevated their social traditions to spiritual truths and Jesus challenged them to change their thinking to better conform to the will of God. Most of the clashes Jesus had with the religious leaders had to do with His violating or justifying the violation of their traditions. He never broke the Law, but they thought He did. The Sermon on the Mount was an iceberg to their Titanic luxury liner of tradition. While we tend to see it as the ultimate call to authentic spirituality, the legalistic Jews saw it as the ultimate call to change. They were screaming, "If it ain't broke, don't fix it," and He was declaring ". . . unless your righteousness surpasses the righteousness of the scribes and Pharisees, you shall not enter the kingdom of heaven" (Matt 5:20). Something was broken and something needed to change.

He told them that true happiness and blessings come from having a godly spirit (Matt 5:3-12). He called for a change in the way they viewed the Law. Keeping and teaching all the Law made one glorify God with good works and desire to be a godly light to the world (vv. 13-20). Four times He emphatically called for change by saying, "You have heard that it was said . . . but I say" (vv. 21,27,33,43). He told them to change the way they treated one another, their customs about adultery, their practice of swearing by things, their spirit of revenge, and even the natural tendency to hate their enemies. He gave what may be the most challenging call for change ever given when He said, "Love your enemies, and pray for those who persecute you" (v. 44). In that day one didn't make friends by telling Jews to love the Romans.

The ultimate Change Agent then commanded, "Beware of practicing your righteousness before men to be noticed by them . . . you have no reward" (Matt 6:1). Jesus commanded them to change the way they gave alms, prayed, and fasted. All these things were to be done privately, consistently, and from the heart. It was a call to keep things on a spiritual level and not continue the tradition of being showy and seeking the praises of man (vv. 2-24). He even had the nerve to tell them to stop worrying! Worry comes from material concerns and social comparisons. He said to forget about those things, because God will take care of those who seek Him (vv. 25-34).

The next call for change was in the realm of judging others. The challenge was clear — stop it! And the way to do that was to zero in on our own personal shortcomings, which would keep us too busy to notice anyone else's faults (Matt 7:1-6). The closing points of His sermon are a flurry of calls for change. Instead of judging others, start praying more; rather than follow the world like most people do, find the narrow way that leads to life; forget the false prophets and just bear good fruit; don't just talk religion, walk it; and stop building your faith on unstable foundations, but build your spiritual house on the Rock ("these words of Mine," vv. 13-29).

If there has been a more radical call for change in any sermon ever preached since the beginning of time, I don't know when it was. There are very few things that Jesus didn't totally change from the Old Covenant to the New. More than anything else, He finalized, once and for all, that faith/religion is a heart-level relationship with God. He virtually destroyed any semblance of outward or showy religion, except to the extent that the outward display originates in the heart of the believer.

With that said, what would Jesus say about our formal, traditional, unchangeable hour of worship on Sunday? How many times would He say, "You have heard it said by men of old . . . but I say?" How many passages from His Sermon on the Mount would He apply to our assemblies? Would He use some of these:

Blessed are the pure in heart, for they shall see God (5:8).

Let your light shine before men in such a way that they may see your good works, and glorify your Father who is in heaven. (5:16).

Everyone who is angry with his brother shall be guilty (5:22).

If therefore you are presenting your offering at the altar, and there remember that your brother has something against you, leave . . . be reconciled to your brother. (5:23-24).

Whoever slaps you on your right cheek, turn to him the other also. (5:39).

And whoever shall force you to go one mile, go with him two. (5:41).

And if you greet your brothers only, what do you do more than others? (5:47).

Beware of practicing your righteousness before men. (6:1).

And when you are praying, do not use meaningless repetition (6:7).

If you do not forgive men, then your Father will not forgive your transgressions. (6:15).

For where your treasure is, there will your heart be also. (6:21).

And why are you so anxious about clothing? (6:28).

Do not judge lest you be judged yourselves. (7:1).

First take the log out of your own eye. (7:5).

Ask, and it shall be given to you. (7:7).

Whatever you want others to do for you, do so for them (7:12).

Not everyone who says to Me, 'Lord, Lord,' will enter the kingdom of heaven; but he who does the will of My Father who is in heaven. (7:21).

Everyone who hears these words of Mine, and acts upon them, may be compared to a wise man. (7:24).

These are just a few of the calls for change Jesus made that can be easily applied to the assembly. In fact, they take on a whole new meaning when that is done. These are no longer just some spiritual challenges to Jews, but a call for true heart-level faith in the life of every Christian. If they can't be applied in the assembly, where can they be applied? I submit that these concepts are just as much a call for radical change in the assembly as they were a call for radical change in the Jews.

If Jesus is the ultimate Change Agent, and He is, and the church is the Body of Christ, which it is, then how can the assembled Body of Christ be anything less than the place of ultimate change? With God's help and one another's encouragement, our primary goal in coming together is to bring about change. We are trying to change the hold that Satan has on our lives. We are trying to change worldly influence on our families. We are trying to change our selfishness into Christlikeness. We are trying to change how unchurched people view the church, the Gospel, and their own spiritual needs. We are trying to change spiritual and numerical decline into spiritual and numerical growth. What does the word "grow" mean if it doesn't mean changing?

Beware of ridiculing change. Beware of labeling those who question the sanctity of the status quo. Beware of fighting to preserve traditions just because you don't like change. Beware of defending a worship style that brings comfort to the few and ignores the decades of spiritual and numerical decline it caused. Beware of putting a higher premium on security and predictability than you do on growing in Christ. Defending the favorite is not the same thing as defending the faith! To stand in the way of needed change is to stand in the way of Jesus.

CHANGE FOR CHANGE'S SAKE

Jesus was, is, and always will be in the change business. He wants us to change from darkness to light, to exchange our burden for His yoke, and to deny ourselves and accept His cross. The New Testament is filled with such descriptions and analogies. No self-respecting Christian would disagree with that spiritual fact for a minute. Do we ever stop changing? Not if we are growing! Are we supposed to stay babes in Christ all our lives, or grow into spiritually mature adults? Everyone knows that we are changing constantly as we become more Christlike. So why are so many so upset about change?

Let's put this problem in perspective. Brethren aren't fussing about Bible classes, benevolence programs, youth ministries, missionary work, evangelism, visitation programs, budgets, VBS, workshops, family ministries, singles programs, office administration, Bible Hours, Young Married's ministries, widows, or Children's Homes. No one is uptight about what happens on Monday, Tuesday, Wednesday, Thursday, Friday, or on Saturday. No one cares about the things you do on Sunday afternoon. You could change nearly everything in the whole wide world, but don't touch that one hour on Sunday morning we call worship. That's what folks are up in arms about.

We have no complete example of a New Testament assembly. One element, the communion, can be called a commanded assembly event, and all the rest are either examples or implied from Scripture. The word worship is never once in Scripture applied to the Christian assembly, and there is as much about day-to-day meeting as there is about Sunday meetings. Yet, we are convinced that we've got it all correct and the way we do it is the only way it can be done. It has become the most important religious hour of the entire week and we dare not change a single thing that we've been doing, even if we've only been doing it for the last half century.

There are several reasons for the preeminence of the Sunday morning assembly in our religion, but very few of them are biblical. The primary reason is tradition. Sure, the early Christians met on the first day of the week to break bread and to lay by in store as they were prospered, but it's twenty centuries of tradition that has made "going to church" on Sunday morning the most important religious event of the week. It's the same twenty centuries of tradition that have created the strong aversion to change that many have, which in turn causes many to blur the distinction between Scripture and custom.

We need some radical changes in our thinking. As mentioned in the section on why the assembly is a battleground, as long as folks continue to see the Sunday morning assembly as the primary religious focus of the week, they will fight anything that looks like change. But we must change. Paul said that we need to "be transformed by the renewing of" our minds (Rom 12:2). What is transformation if it isn't change? In fact, transformation is "change for change's sake." The most often used criticism of change by traditionalists is that it's only "change for change's sake," and somehow that diminishes the need or purpose for the change. What they are doing is arguing for conformity, which is what Paul was warning against when he called for us to be transformed.

When my son was little he had some toys called Transformers. These were toys that could be changed into something else. Some were cars that transformed into planes and others were rocket ships that transformed into robots. They were Transformers because they changed into something else. If they hadn't changed, they wouldn't have been the real thing.

Brethren, we are transformers. We are renewing our minds constantly as we seek to "prove what the will of God is, that which is good and acceptable and perfect." If we are not transformers/changers, we are not in touch with the will of God and hence, not good, acceptable, or perfect (complete).

We must change for change's sake, but spiritual change is change for Christ's sake. It may just begin with understanding that the Sunday morning assembly should not be so protected, so preeminent, and so supremely sacred.

I am sure that sounds heretical to some, but I have stated it strongly to make the point clear. I am not saying that the Sunday morning worship assembly is not important or valuable. There is just nothing in Scripture that gives it the focus that we traditionally give it. God wants us to be together because He wants us to grow in love, unity, and must importantly, in Christ. But because of the lofty position we give to that one assembly we insure resistance to change and the inevitable conflicts that will follow.

As I have mentioned before, I believe it's more biblically accurate to think of the Christian assembly as a tool given by God to be used for spiritual growth. The Body of Christ is like a car that needs maintaining and improving. God has given us many types of tools to use to help tune it up. There are tools like prayer, study, giving, serving, sacrificing, and even trials. Then there is the tool of togetherness, where encouragement and edification build us up as we build others up. Communion, prayer, preaching, singing, and many other parts of the tool, are used to recharge and refit one another so that individually and collectively we will run the race set before us even better.

But, the tool is not the car. It is used to improve the car, not to replace it. Also, it is not any more important than the other tools; however, when you need it, there's nothing like it. Maybe that is why God put so few restrictions on how and when it could be used. It's an amazing tool. It's flexible yet powerful, and it can change lives when used properly. It must be used, however, and not polished and kept in the tool box to protect it from wear and tear. It's a tool that is used to bring about change.

So what have we said? First, Jesus expects change. Second, Christians are changers. Third, the Christian assembly is not TOO important to change, and is in fact a tool to be used for change. The tool itself must not be worshiped, but the God who created it is worshiped when it is used as He intended for it to be used. We must not fear change, even change in the assembly. Fear of change is one of Satan's most powerful devices, because if he can stop change he can stop growth, and when he stops growth he wins.

DISCUSSION QUESTIONS

1. What does it mean to be "a Change Agent?"

2. When does change or tradition become wrong?

3. Was Jesus a Traditionalist or a Change Agent?

4. What are some principles in the Sermon on the Mount (Matt 5–7) that can be applied to the assembly?

5. Why are so many people upset about change in the assembly?

CHAPTER 13
Radical Change

How does the title of this chapter grab you? There are few terms that send chills up the spine of religious people like "radical change." Did you realize that "radical change" is a redundancy? Radical means "favoring extreme change."[20] To say radical change is saying the same thing twice and might even be construed as a double negative. An extreme change change would be a non-extreme change. I told you I enjoy words.

Radical, like liberal or conservative, is a relative term. What constitutes radical thinking to you completely depends on where you are. For most people, a radical is anyone who espouses a more extreme change than they themselves are comfortable with. A radical in the midst of radicals is a moderate. A moderate may, however, be a radical to an ultraconservative, who views all radicals as the antichrist. On the other hand, if one's radical beliefs and actions are a reflection of a silent majority they may very well be called a hero, which is what we call George Washington, Samuel Adams, and the other leaders of the American Revolution. To some, Jesus was a poor carpenter. To others, He was a rabbi, a prophet, a political threat, or a religious radical. To Peter, He was "the Christ, the Son of the living God (Matt 16:14-16). It all depended on where people stood in relation to Him.

I guess I am a radical because I am in favor of extreme change. In fact, I am in favor of total change. Not a change in biblical precepts, but a change back to biblical precepts. It's time to start worshiping God with our lives and not just one hour on Sunday. Worship is total. Just as a lamb's life sacrificed on the altar was total, so our living sacrifice is total. It's the only worship that is acceptable to God.

Listen to a biblical description of radical worship by Paul:

> If then you have been raised up with Christ, keep seeking the things above, where Christ is, seated at the right hand of God. Set your mind on the things above, not on the things that are on earth. For you have died and your life is hidden with Christ in God. When Christ, who is our life, is revealed, then you also will be revealed with Him in glory (Col 3:1-4).

This is a call for total change and for total worship. This passage is saturated with the language of worship. What is worship if it's not "seeking the things above, where Christ is"? Christians do it all the time; they don't just seek Him on Sunday morning. It's our mindset! How total is it to "have died" and have our life "hidden with Christ?" Yet one would dare say that if you miss "church" you miss an opportunity to be with Jesus! "Christ is our life" and we spend every waking moment anticipating our being revealed with Him in glory. That's real, radical worship!

In our life of worship we "consider the members of [our] earthly body as dead to immorality, impurity, passion, evil desire, and greed, which amounts to idolatry" (Col 3:5). This isn't just "Christian living"; it's our living sacrifice of worship to God. These are not just things we don't do on Sunday. We have "put on the new self who is being renewed to a true knowledge according to the image of the One who created" us. This is present tense, ongoing, and never ending! "Christ is all and in all" so we have "a heart of compassion, kindness, humility, gentleness, and patience." We bear with one another and forgive one another as a way of life because He forgave us.

We "put on love, which is the perfect bond of unity," not once a week, or occasionally, but permanently. "The peace of Christ" rules our hearts and "the word[s] of Christ richly dwell within" us every moment of every day, and this causes us to inspire and teach each other with songs of thanksgiving that originate from our hearts. And, whatever we do "in word or deed" we "do all in the name of the Lord Jesus, giving thanks through Him to God the Father." (See Col 3:5-17.) This is real, radical worship!

This great passage in Colossians says nothing about Sunday, but it says everything about living worship. It's time for extreme change — it's time to start recognizing that "whatever you do" you do it in the name of Jesus. Whenever — wherever! Can something that is done in the name of Jesus not be worship? Can you give "thanks through Him to God the Father" and it not be worshiping?

There is not the slightest doubt in my mind that to Paul, worship was a life given in obedience to God, or, to use his words, a "life hidden with Christ in God." That's radical worship!

We must change our traditional definition of worship as only something we do on Sunday morning. Not only is it unbiblical and limiting, it completely misses the larger purpose of worship. Real worship is reflecting the attributes of God in our life.

Except for a very few minor instances, in the New

Testament praise and worship are synonymous terms, as I've already pointed out. Praise is reflecting positively on or about God, like Paul said, "we...should be to the praise of His glory" (Eph 1:12). Likewise, worship is reflecting positively on or about God in either word or deed. How do we reflect positively on God? By being godly, or manifesting His attributes in our lives.

The simplest way to understand and measure this concept in our lives is to ask ourselves, "To what extent do I reflect the fruit of the Spirit in my life?" The fruit of the Spirit, as given to us in Galatians 5:22-25, is the prescription for what "a living sacrifice" is all about, and hence, worship. How do we know that it's referring to our living sacrifice? It is because of how Paul concludes his thoughts on the fruit of the Spirit. He said, "Now those who belong to Christ Jesus have **crucified the flesh** with its passions and desires." One doesn't need a Ph.D. in Theology to recognize that a living crucifixion is the same thing as a living sacrifice. They are synonymous analogies. He then adds, "If we **live by the Spirit**, let us also **walk by the Spirit**." Again, living and walking are synonyms for a life totally given to God.

Each characteristic of the fruit of the Spirit is an attribute of God that He wants us to internalize and live by. When we have these in our life, we reflect positively on God and worship Him. Love may be the single greatest act of worship there is. God is love, and those who are filled with love are godly. Showing love for one another is the single most important proof there is that we belong to Him. It is the evidence that convicts us of discipleship, it binds us together, and it covers a multitude of sins.

Joy is an act of worship. You wouldn't know that in most of our assemblies, but it is an integral part of our faith. As Peter put it, "though you have not seen Him, you love Him, and though you do not see Him now, but **believe in Him**, you **greatly rejoice with joy inexpress-**

ible and full of glory" (1 Pet 1:8). Paul made it an imperative when he said, "**Rejoice in the Lord always; and again I will say rejoice**" (Phil 4:4). It is an inseparable part of the Christian life that remains in good times and bad times. It doesn't require external or material justification because it is the condition of the Christian heart, and we don't hang it on the coat rack when we enter the church building. It is the reflection of a God-centered life.

Is your church family in turmoil over what style of worship assembly to have? Are you torn with anxiety over wanting to keep your older, more traditional members happy, but not wanting to lose any more Boomers, Busters, and teens? What's the solution? Real worship! The kind that begins and ends in your heart regardless of what everyone else wants or does in the church building. It's the "**peace of God, which surpasses all comprehension**." It's not apathy or cynicism. It's not a cop-out rationale. It's the peace that only comes from God, and it's the only peace that "shall guard your hearts and your minds in Christ Jesus" (Phil 4:7). That's real worship! You never go to it or leave it — you're it!

One of the most powerful evidences of God being present in our lives is patience. It is a concrete sign of spiritual maturity and it reflects mightily on God. Why? I would venture to say that it is nearly impossible to care passionately about something and still be able to be patient about it without the help of God.

On several occasions I have been sitting in the Sunday morning assembly and seen brethren get red-faced, cross-armed, and head-shaking mad about something different being done. Not something unscriptural, just something different. I knew they were mad, and I knew they would fuss-up-a-storm to an elder, and I knew the chances were good that the "something different" would be outlawed in the future. It had something to do with "a squeaking wheel" proverb. My stomach was in knots. My head ached.

My hands perspired. And I had to get up and preach, looking that brother in the eye, as if everything was wonderful. So I prayed and asked God, "What would Jesus do if He were in my position?" A good idea was going to be canned, a lot of folks on both sides of the issue were going to be upset, and truthfully, I was more than miffed. Then I visualized Jesus sitting in my spot on the front pew. I saw His relaxed posture and peaceful face. Most of all I saw Him smile. Everything about Him said, "Be patient." Now my motto is "Relax and smile — it's in His hands." That is a heart-level commitment that reflects on God every time I remember it, whether I'm in heavy traffic, a heavy discussion, or heavy with frustration. Relax and smile! Be patient! That's real worship!

Why would anyone feel threatened to discover that worship is a way of life and not just one hour Sunday morning? Isn't it inspiring to think about God being worshiped by millions every second of every day? Isn't it thrilling to know that acts of worship are being performed all over the world, all day every day and not just within the walls of a church building? Every time someone displays an attribute of God — **He is worshiped!** Every act of **kindness, goodness, faithfulness, gentleness, and self-control** goes up to God as a fragrant offering of worship and praise. Just think about how many times today you have worshiped God. Look at that list of Spiritual fruit and remember how many times today you have been kind, good, obedient, gentle, or self-controlled. These are all things that you do naturally, as a way of life, just because God has made a difference in your life. **Praise the Lord!** Isn't it wonderful to realize that you are a walking, talking, worshiping child of a King?

Don't miss that hour, or two or three, on Sunday, but don't see your worship to God only from the standpoint of what does or doesn't happen then. Whether you want massive changes in your Sunday morning assembly or whether you want everything to stay just like it was when you were a kid, don't let your focus on that one hour destroy your life of worship to God. If you have the oldest, most boring one hour of endurance in your assembly on Sunday morning, with five-hundred-year-old songs and a century-old order of worship, God will still be looking for your life to reflect His attributes and thereby glorify Him — every hour of every day — including that one hour on Sunday morning. In fact, if you can't reflect those godly attributes for that one hour, when can you? They're required even when (especially when) we don't get our way!

The reason we need a radical change in our understanding of worship is because we need a radical change in how we view our Christian walk. This is a much bigger need than changing our assembly style or fighting to keep it unchanged. The significance of recognizing that worship is our life is not that it paves the way for radical changes in our assembly, but that it holds us to a higher standard than being mere churchgoers.

DISCUSSION QUESTIONS

1. What does it mean to be radical?

2. Would it require a radical change for us to worship like they did in the New Testament?

3. What does it mean that "worship is reflecting the attributes of God?"

4. Could it be said that exhibiting the fruit of the Spirit is an act of worship?

5. What is spiritual integrity?

CHAPTER 14
What Difference Does It Make?

You're doing your income taxes all by yourself and you remember that you did some work for a friend who paid you in cash. Should you include it as income on your tax form, or conveniently ignore it? After all, no one will know.

It's four o'clock in the morning and you have a long drive ahead of you. There's no traffic on the road, but there you sit, alone, at a stop light. You could bust right through it and no one would see it. After all, you're a law-abiding driver most of the time.

You've been away from home for a week now on a business trip. You're lonely, bored, and discouraged. An attractive gal who's staying at the same hotel has really been "coming on" to you, and you're starting to think, "Hey, no one will ever know if . . . ."

Someone once said, "Integrity is what you are when no one is looking." It is the inner character that directs you to do what's right simply because it's right and not because of what others think or do. Someone else once said that "Integrity is the gift you give yourself." It's the good feeling of being good.

Worship is spiritual integrity. It's a quality of the heart that demands higher priorities and complete consistency. We desperately need men and women with spiritual integrity who don't leave their worship to God in the foyer of the church building like a pair of bowling shoes left in a locker at the bowling alley. It makes a big difference when we recognize that our worship to God takes place wherever we are, and we will be held accountable for ignoring it — even when no one is looking. As you know, One is always looking.

Understanding that worship is our life makes a big difference in that it destroys segmented living. We tend to think of our lives as having several segments. We have a family, a job, recreation or hobbies, and we have church. These are not only areas of our lives that we struggle to keep properly prioritized, but they are often areas of life where we are completely different people in each one. Are you the dedicated family man (or woman) who is ruthless and cutthroat in your business? Maybe you're the church deacon who is so dependable and loving at church, but who consistently gets thrown out of the church league softball game for unsportsmanlike conduct. There are plenty of folks who patiently and compassionately deal with customers all day at work, then snap at their kids and ignore them each evening when they get home.

Where you see the most inconsistency is in the group of people who attend "worship" on Sunday morning, where they sing, pray, give, commune, and study God's Word, then leave "worship" never to mention the name of Jesus all week except as an expletive. To them church is something good people go to; after all, the kids need it, and it's not much different than a community club or a civic duty.

They leave church feeling that they have done their worshiping for the week and now it's time to continue with the real world.

We may judgmentally call these folks "churchgoers," "pew sitters," "marginal members," or even hypocrites, but they are doing what we told them to do. They've gone to church, they've paid their dues, and they've had their "good person" ticket punched for another week. They've been to "worship," but unfortunately they left it right where they found it, and they've taken care of that segment of their lives.

Brethren need to know that they can't walk away from worship. It goes with them wherever they go. They worship God by being trustworthy, Christlike employees, loving and involved parents and spouses, good sports and encouragers, and by wanting to assemble with other Christians in order to "stir one another to love and good works." Their worship is like their integrity; it reflects the character of their hearts.

In a passage we've looked at already we saw that "Jesus kept increasing in wisdom and stature, and in favor with God and men" (Luke 2:52). These were different areas of His life, but He consistently grew in each one and He was still Jesus, the Son of God in each one. Can you imagine Jesus acting differently depending on who He happened to be with at the time? Can you imagine Him treating people differently? Christ can't be un-Christlike, and neither should Christians. The traditional approach to worship contributes to this segmented living and it cheapens the consistency that God demands in our lives.

Christians need more than the admonition on the church auditorium door that they "Enter to worship. Leave to serve." Worship is the motivation to serve as well as the service itself. The intent of the heart and the act of service are both offerings of worship to God. We have no right nor biblical authority to segment worship and service. They are like faith and works; one is dead without the other. Besides, it is far more biblically accurate and productive to have a sign that says, "Enter to serve. Leave to worship."

Life worship can make a big difference in the life of a husband and dad. The faith, hope, and love that he sings about on Sunday morning needs to be seen in the spiritual leadership he shows his wife and children every day. They desperately need to see that God has made a difference in his life because they see him offer up a life of worship to God constantly. They need to see genuine religion from their father, who first and foremost wants them in heaven with him. Few things do more to destroy the faith of children as they grow than to see a dichotomy in Dad's life. They quickly learn that this church stuff is a facade, and Jesus is like Santa Claus — an idea that you grow too old to believe in.

Life worship can make a big difference in the life of a wife and mother too. Kindness and sweetness are not just gender-specific values. Some wives and mothers are naturally that way, but the truly godly women have a special kind of love that sticks in the hearts of their husbands and children for eternity. Too often moms provide the only spiritual leadership in the home, and too often, they feel like it's not enough or it's not that important. Christian women need to know that their expressions of loving kindness, no matter how small or insignificant they seem, are acts of worship to God. It's the cumulative effect of all that love, offered to God in the name of Jesus, that often helps save the very souls of their children. A mother's love is powerful, essential, life-changing, and worship to God!

One of the most dangerous things a dad and mom can do to their children is to turn over the spiritual nurturing of their children to the church. It was never God's intent that the church raise your children "in the nurture and admonition of the Lord." This is not taking anything away from our church programs, but if you leave your child's spiritual training up to a forty-five-minute Bible class, once a week, followed by an hour long period of sheer boredom in the assembly (from a child's standpoint), then don't be surprised when they stop going to church the first week of their freshman year at college. Even the best Sunday morning Bible class is nothing more than a supplement to what you should be teaching at home. I'm not talking about adding lengthy, daily Bible study to your schedule as a parent, though some of that wouldn't be a bad idea. I am talking about recognizing that everything you do at home with your family is, or should be, reflecting God. Your hugs, story telling, singing, prayers, talking, teaching, encouraging, rolling around on the floor together, meals, trips, kisses, and Christlike example are worship. It's all in the name of Jesus, to the glory of God, and it's living to His praise. It's some of the best worship you will ever be part of.

I have three wonderful, godly children that I thank God for every day. I can guarantee you that they are not that way because their mother and I preached to them or forced Scripture down their throats regularly. They are that way because we loved them — a lot — and we showed them in everything we did that we loved God. There never was a social life, a school life, a career life and a church life — there was only our life in Christ, and all of it was worship to God. Go to church together! It's a wonderful family affair. Read your Bibles, pray, and tell Bible stories to your children. But more than anything else, let them see Jesus in your lives in everything you do.

One of the greatest gifts that you can give your children is to help them understand that they are worshiping God wherever they go, whatever they do, and whoever they are with. Don't provide them with the rationale they might some day seek to place their religion into a segment of their lives. Life worship can make a big difference in their lives.

Just think what a difference it could make in the lives of Christian teenagers to understand that they are living to the praise of God. When peer pressure is strong to experiment with drugs, join in on the beer bash, or be sexually promiscuous, they may just remember that these are deeds that can't be done to the glory of God or in the name of Jesus. They may just have enough faith to get their self-esteem from God and not from being accepted by the other kids. They just might be able to refuse segmented living that has them being one person with the church youth group, but an entirely different person at school. If they can accept the fact that worship is what they are instead of what they go to once a week, they may just be able to have a real prayer life of their own and develop a personal relationship with the Father.

IT IS THE RIGHT DIFFERENCE

Not only does worship as a way of life make a big difference in how we live, but it helps us be consistent and accurate in our biblical concepts. No longer can we separate worship and godly living. Godly living is a life given in obedience to God and is therefore worship. No longer can we separate worship and setting the right example. Worship is setting the right example. As mentioned before, we can't separate service and worship any more than we can separate worship and praise, or worship and glorifying God.

I am convinced that the biggest reason why some folks are threatened by the idea of worship being our life and not just our Sunday morning assembly is that it destroys the convenient departmentalizing of our theology that we have created. This has already been dealt with elsewhere in this book, but man created the concept of a formal and informal worship. Man created the idea of horizontal versus vertical worship. These are traditions of man that allow us to bind biblical concepts in one area and unbind them in the other. The fear is that if we don't make a distinction in worship, there will be religious anarchy and confusion. It's comfortable, convenient, and seemingly consistent to conclude that some things are required only in the formal assembly, but may not be necessary in informal worship, or in the privacy of your home.

There must be consistent application of biblical truths. That is a fact! If worship is your life, and you determine from the Bible that something cannot be part of your worship, then that must be consistently applied. Don't use a man-made concept, like formal worship, to justify something you want to do. For example, many brethren believe that the use of instrumental music in worship is unbiblical, and all their singing is a cappella. But many of those same people believe that singing a hymn with a piano in their home is okay, because it's "not the formal worship." Again, that is convenient and comfortable, but it's not biblical. When is "singing with thanksgiving in your heart to God" not worship? When is "teaching and admonishing one another with psalms and hymns and spiritual songs" not worship? Is it the magical opening and closing prayer that makes the difference? Where do you find that in the Bible?

Please understand that I am not discussing the rights or wrongs of instrumental music. I'll save that for other people to write about. That doesn't take anything away from the point being made. There is absolutely no reason why understanding worship as our life should change any other doctrinal conclusions about acceptable worship, but it may mean that we start consistently applying it.

Another major area where applying living worship seems to frighten brethren is in determining the role of women in worship. Traditionally, we have said that Paul's admonition in 1 Corinthians 14:34 and 1 Timothy 2:11, for women to be silent in the church, was referring to the formal assembly. Again, before the opening prayer and after the closing prayer, they can talk their heads off, but during that formal worship hour, they must be silent (except for singing, congregational readings, and, in some places, a subdued Amen). There is no formal worship in the New Testament. There are only Christians, who are living worship, being together. If you believe that there is a biblical command that women must not speak when men are present, you must apply it consistently. If it's the right doctrine, it's right wherever it must be applied, but don't use a man-made rationale to justify something you don't know how to deal with in any other way. If it doesn't make sense to apply it in a mixed Bible class, what is the justification for applying it in that one hour on Sunday?

In 1 Timothy 2, it is a general instruction for women in the church at Ephesus, and nothing in the passage applies it to a formal assembly. Even in 1 Corinthians 14, where it does mention "If therefore the whole church should assemble together," the context is dealing with breaking bread as a meal, as the Lord's Supper, and as sharing Jesus. Which one of these was Paul limiting the instruction about women to? If you believe that Paul was giving an absolute doctrine for all Christians everywhere and not just dealing with specific first century problems in Corinth and Ephesus, then you must consistently apply that doctrine any time Christians are together in mixed company. Paul said, "Let the women keep silent in the churches; for they are not permitted to speak" (1 Cor 14:34). When are women not "in the churches?" Is he referring to a church as a building? Is he referring to church as "in the formal worship?" Did he understand what a tremendous difference an opening or closing prayer would make in determining when women could speak?

In 1 Corinthians 11:5, women were "praying and prophesying" and the problem was that their heads were not covered. This can be easily explained away as something that was done before the opening prayer and was not a part of the formal worship. Would Paul be comfortable with that explanation? Is it biblical? If our traditional thinking about formal worship is right then it certainly is a possible explanation for why women could speak in one instance but be forbidden in another. All we have to do is find "opening prayer" and "formal worship" in our Bibles somewhere.

The point is that there must be consistency in our doctrines, and life worship helps provide it. Another good example of this is in the area of evangelism. We can say what we want about what evangelism is supposed to be in theory, but because of our traditional approach with the formal Sunday worship and our elevating it to such a prominent place, brethren will always see it as the primary place for evangelism. After all, we want the plan of salvation restated each week, followed by an invitation to respond, and we have paid professionals to do our soul winning. The lack of conversions year in and year out is simply a reflection on how hard-core the sinners are and not our lack of outreach. At least that is our rationale. So we continue doing what we've always done and wonder why our church is declining.

When brethren start realizing that Jesus must be lifted up in their homes, at their jobs, in their neighborhoods, and at their schools, and not just at the church building on Sunday morning, we will start having real evangelism. Our assembly is a "one another" activity that causes us to win another for Christ as a natural part of our life worship to God. The assembly has got to stop being the end result of our religion and start being the causative agent it was meant to be.

We need to minimize the focus on attending worship and emphasize the importance of being worship. This does not mean that we do not need to attend every gathering of the saints, but it does mean that we start using it instead of idolizing it. Because we have a religion of "going to church" we end up believing that the way to help others "get religion" is to get them to "go to church." In essence, we try to convert them to the tool instead of the Truth. People are dying in sin and in desperate need of hearing about Jesus from our lips, but we believe the answer is to just get them to church. That's not evangelism, it's traditionalism gone to seed. If we want others to worship with us they must first see worship in us at the ball field, the backyard, in the lunchroom, breakroom, boardroom, homeroom, or whatever room we happen to be in.

Jesus promised that if He was lifted up, all men would be drawn to Him (John 12:32). He was not only talking about the power of His death and resurrection but our responsibility as lifters. Lifting up Jesus is life worship, not just Sunday morning worship.

I know it sounds heretical to suggest that we minimize the focus on the assembly. So I'm a heretic; but before you break out the tar and feathers, ask yourself what verses from the New Testament would you use to justify the centrality and the preeminence of the assembly in our church life today? Should it be a surprise to anyone that if we turn one small area of the Christian life into a dominant focal point for our religion that other responsibilities might get neglected or ignored? Most of the folks in your congregation have no other ministry that they participate in other than attending THE worship. If you really want to get into trouble, just suggest to them that they need to do something besides "go to church." If you really want to become unpopular, suggest to them that there are things MORE IMPORTANT THAN "church services." (Do not attempt to do this if you happen to derive a salary from said people.)

Maybe the best way to get our spiritual priorities in order is to understand that our entire lives are given in worship to God. We need to understand that Judgment Day will not be The Great Attendance Record Tallying Day, when the final score is totaled up and heaven is awarded to those who prove to have been faithful to the assembly. It will, however, be a day when those who have glorified God by living for Him every hour of their lives, with every word and deed, through every act of compassion and every transforming change of their hearts, will hear the words, "Well done, thou good and faithful servant." They will hear the words "Enter in," not because they didn't forsake the assembly, which they didn't, but because they really worshiped God.

The benefits that come from recognizing that our life is worship to God, and acting upon that truth, are endless; but quite possibly the most important benefit is unity. I don't know of a mid- to large-size congregation that isn't suffering from some kind of disunity because of the assembly. As mentioned in an earlier section of this book, brethren are fighting about changes or the lack of changes in their assembly time. It's a battle over traditions versus new ideas, but it's even more complicated than that. The traditionalists are not any more united about what they want to protect then the new-idea folks are about what they want changed. About the time you think it's totally a generation problem, the young marrieds cry out for the old ways, and some progressive Primetimers cheer for change. What muddies up the water even more is the abuse of Scripture to justify arguments and thus turning the issues into matters of faith and not just preference. Brotherly love gets demoted by the desire to get what we want — what makes us feel good — what we think meets our needs in the assembly. Too often, Jesus gets trashed by traditions and trampled by thoughtless changes.

It doesn't have to be this way and, more importantly, it shouldn't be this way!

DISCUSSION QUESTIONS

1. What difference would it make if Christians started understanding that worship was their life and not just one hour on Sunday morning?

2. How would worship as a lifestyle make us better mates, parents, employees, and friends?

3. How does a formal worship help us departmentalize our theology?

4. Does it change our theology of music or the role of women in the assembly when we understand worship is our life?

5. Why would it be beneficial to minimize our focus on the assembly?

SECTION FIVE
Relevant Worship

CHAPTER 15
New and Old Whine

What would you think about someone who went out to dinner at a fancy restaurant and instead of partaking of fine cuisine they spent the evening reading the wine list? Not only would we be shocked over their missing the whole point of the event, but we'd probably shout "Get a life, will ya!" So what do you say to folks who make a special trip to Break Bread, and not only do they miss the whole point of the event, but they spend their time creating a *whine* list?

You are familiar with the church's "Whine List," aren't you? Here are some of the top offerings, but to get the full effect, you need to raise the pitch of your voice, pinch your nose, and read these out loud.

"When are we going to have a worship that meets my needs?"

"Why can't we just do things the way we always have?"

"Let's sing more new songs!"

"Next thing ya know, they'll want to dance and shout in the aisles!"

"When are we going to have a relevant, Twenty-first Century worship service?"

The list is endless and probably timeless. Somewhere along the path of church history we stopped meeting together to give and started meeting to get. Somewhere we exchanged joyful open hearts for scorecards and a chip on our shoulders, and began analyzing, judging, and criticizing everything that took place in the assembly. As the assembly became the center of our religion, our expectations changed from the simple "It's great to be with brethren," to "It just doesn't do anything for me anymore." Some fear losing their comfort and security while others fear the assembly will become archaic and meaningless. Neither fear has anything to do with the biblical intent of the assembly.

I could write volumes about fear, especially fear associated with worship. I've been labeled a liberal, a heretic, a radical, and a change agent, because I dared challenge people to rethink their traditions. I've been "written up" in articles and rejected for speaking appointments because some thought I was rocking the boat too much. Despite the vow in the introduction to *Spilt Grape Juice* that all I wanted was for people to go back to their Bibles and restudy the subject of worship, and despite my promise at the start of every lesson on worship that I am not seeking to change anything about our assembly style, many are still sure that I have a hidden agenda and I am out to radically change the church.

In fact, I have led several seminars on worship at many churches across the country, and most folks are shocked that I didn't "slap around the traditionalists" and endorse dramatic changes in their assembly. They are even more shocked when I make it clear that unity in Christ is far more important than any change or any tradition. One of my favorite comments to make at seminars is "It's all right to do anything, change or no change, for the sake of unity." It's a waste of time and energy to preach or teach about change, or fight to maintain the status quo, if church members don't have the mind of Christ. When brethren have a spirit of wanting to please Him, and do only what will be best for His will, the changing will take care of itself.

People are screaming for relevant worship. Churches are splitting because some want a more contemporary style while others want things to stay just like they are. Other congregations are offering multiple assemblies with each one having a different style and appealing to different needs in their church family. In some cases it's a wonderful example of wisdom, while in others it's a tribute to intolerance between brethren.

What is relevant worship? What's relevant is relative. Many spiritual things are always relevant, especially things that take place in the heart. If my life is a living sacrifice to God and, therefore, living worship to God, how can worship possibly be irrelevant?

Please understand this important concept! Relevant worship is not and never will be change in the assembly. Relevant worship is change in the heart of a Christian that makes him or her more Christlike.

It's time to stop blaming others for our own lack of commitment to Jesus! If you're walking and talking with Jesus twenty-four hours a day, seven days a week, and what happens that one hour on Sunday doesn't just thrill you to the bone, who cares? You've got Jesus! Is it that terrible to spend an hour letting others be enriched by something that doesn't particularly tickle your fancy? Is there absolutely nothing that you can get out of an assembly that others seem to really enjoy? It really is supposed to be more blessed to give than to receive. Is that not true in the Christian assembly?

If we allow our togetherness to be poisoned by thinking, "Those old folks won't allow us to change anything," or "Those young folks just want change for change's sake," then we have let Satan win a powerful victory. He's worked us up to the point that selfishness rules and Jesus is forgotten. You see, when we understand that our whole life is worship to God, we don't have to have everything we think we want on Sunday. We can help others, who don't understand that worship is more than that one hour, have something that will keep them closer to Jesus. At the same time, we can have the warm feeling of having sacrificed our wants for others we supposedly love more than ourselves. How can that be wrong or bad?

In the last four years, since the publishing of *Spilt Grape Juice*, I have received scores of long distance phone calls from preachers, teachers, and even elders, asking me why it was that they presented the ideas in there about worship, but no one wanted to change. They were surprised that brethren didn't just jump up and overhaul the entire assembly when they heard that all of life was worship. They usually closed by asking me what they needed to do to get their church to change. My answer was always the same, even when the wording was different: Don't worry about changing the assembly; bring about change in their hearts. Lead your congregation in a deeper understanding of what the Bible really says. Keep it nonthreatening. Create an atmosphere of loyalty to the Word and a consistent commitment to the restoration plea. Remind one another that while the truth sets us free, it also empowers us to be submissive, and we are submissive "out of reverence for Christ" (Eph 5:21, KJV).

In the next three chapters of this section I want to suggest three things that we need to do if we want to have relevant worship. The fourth and final chapter of this section and the book will cover some practical challenges for "What to do next."

DISCUSSION QUESTIONS

1. What are some additions to the "whine list" that you could make?

2. As long as spiritual truths are not in question, when does change or tradition become more important than unity?

3. What will always be relevant worship?

CHAPTER 16
Climb a Mountain

What are some of the major turning points in your life —
times when you had a real change take place? Most of us
would naturally think of events like turning sixteen and
starting to drive a car, or graduations from high school or
college. Soon after that, we'd list all the normal things that
everyone would expect, like marriage, having children,
getting a job, and maybe later, changing jobs and moving
to a new part of the country.

What about significant spiritual changes in your life;
when did they occur? Of course your conversion was a significant life-changing experience, but what about since
then? Has there been a time of renewal, rededication, or
recommitment? Was there a period when you did some
serious soul-searching and had a change of heart and a
change in direction? Have you experienced what I call
"spiritual grieving," when you really struggle with what
God wants you to be or do, an experience which usually
lasts several days?

I really don't know how a person could possibly live with the Lord for a number of years and not go through several periods of self-examination, which become pivotal turning points in their spiritual growth. God expects this. Paul was talking about this process when he said,

> Now the Lord is the Spirit; and where the Spirit of the Lord is, there is liberty. But we all, with unveiled face beholding as in a mirror the glory of the Lord, are being transformed into the same image from glory to glory, just as from the Lord, the Spirit (2 Cor 3:17-18).

This is not a forced change, because in the Lord "there is liberty," but it is an expected change. As we are confronted by our need to be like Him in spirit, we are "being transformed" or changed into something special. What is the "image" that we are being transformed into? It's the image of the Lord! He constantly works on our hearts and molds them into His image, but we must WANT it to happen — we are at liberty to refuse it! That is why we need those special personal crisis times in our lives. They are times when we renew our desire to be like Him.

We need to regularly climb a mountain with Jesus. It's the place where we can walk and talk with Him and even argue as we speak the truth in love. It's where we confess our weaknesses and profess our dependence on Him. Sometimes it involves being alone with Him, but other times it means to be with His people.

You remember the first recorded trip Jesus made up the mountain, don't you? I think of it as a mountain even though the Scriptures call it a wilderness, because He was "led up by the Spirit," and there also seemed to be "a very high mountain" close by that Satan used to tempt Him. The wilderness was a barren, mountainous area where one could easily be alone. He was about thirty years old, fresh from His baptism by John, and ready to begin His ministry that would end on a cross. We usually refer to this as The

Temptations of Jesus, but it was more than a fight with Satan. It was a turning point in His life that marked the beginning of the end of His long absence from Home, and His change from being a simple carpenter to a mansion builder for us.

The story starts by saying ". . . Jesus was led up by the Spirit into the wilderness to be tempted by the devil. And after He had fasted forty days and forty nights, He then became hungry." This is followed by the three encounters with Satan, who tempts Jesus to break His fast, test God, and sell out to him. Satan is scorned and rebuked with Scripture. "Then the devil left Him; and behold, angels came and began to minister to Him." (See Matt 4:1-11.).

I see Jesus going up that mountain to do four things. First, it was a **Retreat**. Not that He was running away from anything, but a retreat in the sense that He did need to get away. Jesus was the supreme people person, but He regularly needed to get away. Sometimes He used a mountain, while other times it was a garden or a boat, or someone's home. Sometimes He was totally alone and other times He was with just a few people, but it was always a time when He could break out of the routine, the grind of the task at hand, and think.

We need to go up that mountain and retreat with Jesus. We need it! We need to break free from our ruts and our comfort zones and have a time when we can uncloud our brains and think — pray — examine — pray some more. Sometimes we need to be totally alone with Him so we can do as the old song says, ". . . and He walks with me and He talks with me, and He tells me I am His own." Sure, we "pray without ceasing," but we also need some "closet time" or kneeling time, when we meditate without distraction.

Sometimes we need to retreat with Jesus' people. After all, they are His body! He lives in them! They are not only His followers, but they are His brothers and sisters, fellow heirs of God, who have been adopted into His family — like you have. You can't afford to miss a retreat like that. Of course you live to worship Jesus, but what a thrill it is to get together with other worshipers and just get away from the world for a while. What a joy to retreat into the family of God and think about nothing else but how great God is and how wonderful it is to serve Him as a family. It's just being together that counts — that's what makes it a retreat with Jesus. Everything else is just incidental. Retreating with Jesus, now that's relevant worship!

The second reason why Jesus went up the mountain was to **Refocus**. I certainly don't mean to suggest that Jesus ever got sidetracked, but it was time for Him to totally turn His attention to His mission. His nail apron was hanging in the shop, the sawdust had been shaken off, and His duties as head of His family had been turned over to a younger sibling. Now He had only one task, reconciling man back to God. In humble submissiveness He'd agreed to this sacrifice long before man even needed it, but He needed to refocus on all the reasons why it had to be done and why He accepted the mission.

We need to be with Jesus and refocus on His mission. In fact, He specifically told us to do certain things "in remembrance of Me." We need to refocus on the awesome love that motivated Him to leave heaven, exchange His spiritual body for a mortal one, and wake up every morning for about thirty-three years knowing the cross was waiting for Him. We need to talk! "How could you do it, Jesus? How could you love me so much when I am so sinful? How could you forgive me, when I ignored you for so long? How can your blood continue to wash away my sins without me even knowing it? How can I be more like you?" Then we need to listen! He will answer every question. He'll use His word, or have someone guide you to the answer, or He may just let you grow into the right answer. Whatever way Jesus uses to talk to us requires that we be in communication with Him.

Isn't it wonderful that being with His people causes us to refocus on Him? We are all "fixing our eyes on Jesus," individually, and receiving encouragement from one another to stay focused on Him so we won't become blind or shortsighted. That is why God wants us to be together, that is the purpose of the assembly, and that is why we need each other. We have a personal relationship with Jesus, and He promised to be with us and help us always, but He also gave us a powerful tool in Christian together-ness to assist us in this task. We can't see Jesus in the lives of other Christians, and they can't see Him in us, if we are not together. And we can't be identified as His disciples if the world doesn't see us love one another.

The third reason why Jesus went up the mountain for forty days and forty nights was to **Renew** His relationship with God. Not renew in the sense that it had weakened, but a renewal of love, commitment, and unity. He showed His love for God by answering Satan's challenge to His Sonship with the declaration that man lives "on every word that pro-ceeds out of the mouth of God." Later He would tell His dis-ciples that to love meant obedience to God and He proved that in His own life. When Satan questioned His commit-ment to that obedience by tempting Him to test God, He responded, "You shall not tempt the Lord your God."

The last thing Satan tried to do was destroy the unity between the Father and the Son by tempting Jesus to follow his plan for winning the world. All He had to do was worship Satan and all the kingdoms of the world would be given to Him. Not only was that the wrong plan, but he was the wrong one to worship, and Jesus told him so. He said, "Begone, Satan! For it is written, 'You shall worship the Lord your God, and serve only Him." Thus Jesus recon-firmed all the elements of His relationship with His Father and dealt firmly with Satan. He renewed for Himself and for all mankind the simple truth that God must be wor-shiped and Satan must be rejected.

We need that mountain experience with Jesus. We need Him to help us renew our relationship with the true and living God, who planned for our salvation before He even created the heavens and the earth. We need Him to help us recommit to God when the fires of love in our heart begin to cool down. We need His help in dealing with Satan's relentless attacks. We need His words to be on our lips so we will have the right answers to fight back with. We want to live godly lives, and "His divine power has granted to us everything pertaining to life and godliness;" which we can only get "through the true knowledge of Him" (2 Pet 1:3). That means we must spend time with Him, know Him, trust Him, and love Him completely.

Praise the Lord, He has an army of servants who want to help us. He wants us to be with others who want to live for Him just like us. He wants us to help each other renew our relationship with God. The New Testament Christians did it "day to day" and "from house to house." They met together to encourage one another to grow in their relationship with God and to equip one another to deal with Satan. Christians should leave their time spent together renewed in their resolve to live for Jesus. That is relevant worship.

The final reason why Jesus went up the mountain was to **Rearm**. Again, I don't mean to suggest that He was unarmed or powerless. He was the Son of God before He went up the mountain, but He got help from the Spirit, who led Him up there. Was that a miraculous transporting of Jesus from the river Jordan to the mountaintop, or was it a sensitivity to the Spirit's guidance? I think the latter is the correct conclusion. The Spirit was helping Him prepare for Satan's attack. And speaking of spiritual weaponry, did you notice what Jesus used to deal with Satan? He had Satan out-gunned! He used Scripture, prayer, and meditation. Neither man or Satan has ever developed a more powerful weapon than any one of these three. No wonder "the devil left Him."

We need to spend time with Jesus getting rearmed. We need to follow His example and use Scripture, prayer, and meditation to defeat Satan every time he tries to move in on our lives. The reason why so many are weak and unable to withstand the darts of the evil one is because they are out of ammunition. Jesus can change that, if we only spend enough time with Him.

You know what is really amazing? Paul told us all to "take up the full armor of God, that you may be able to resist in the evil day, and having done everything, to stand firm" (Eph 6:13-18). He compared our armaments to a soldier's armor and weapons, but it's the same stuff Jesus used (stuff is a technical term for items). You know the list:

Loins girded with truth
The breastplate of righteousness
Feet shod with the preparation of the Gospel of peace
The shield of faith
The helmet of salvation
The sword of the Spirit
With all prayer and petition

Look at that list again. Everything on it fits into one of the three things Jesus did. They either come from Scripture/study, prayer, or meditation (contemplating and internalizing His word). It worked for Him, and it will work for us.

Not only will Jesus personally help us rearm for battle, but He will use His followers to help us too. It's called equipping in the New Testament. "He gave some as apostles, and some as prophets, and some as evangelists, and some as pastors and teachers, for the equipping of the saints for the work of service, to the building up of the body of Christ" (Eph 4:11-12). A major reason why Christians must get together regularly is to rearm one another spiritually. We need regular doses of love, forgiveness, fellowship, admonitions, rebukes, insights, challenges, encouragement, and an opportunity to return the favor. We need to be on the mountain alone with Jesus, but He also wants us on the mountain with our brethren, His family, His disciples. That's relevant worship.

This may seem like an inappropriate parallel to make because Jesus went up on the mountain to be alone. But He really wasn't alone was He? The Spirit was there and so was the Father. After all, who was He talking to in His prayers? Satan was there also. I suspect he likes to catch us alone when no one is around to encourage us to do what's right. Still, the reason why the parallel fits the idea of us not only being alone with Jesus, but alone with our brethren, is because the church is One Body — it's the Body of Christ. We need time to be alone with Jesus, but also time to be alone with His Body, the church.

It's a mystery that was hidden for ages, but Paul revealed it as "Christ in you, the hope of glory" (Col 1:26-27). God wants us to be with others who have Christ in them, because that gives us a chance to be with Christ Himself. When you rub shoulders with a bunch of folks who have that "hope of glory," some of it is going to rub off on you. This is one of the ways that the goal of helping "every man [to be] complete in Christ" will be fulfilled (Col 1:28).

To summarize, relevant worship is having a relationship with Jesus where we can retreat, refocus, renew, and rearm with His help. One of the main ways that we are with Jesus is to be with His people and share the job of retreating from the world, refocusing on Him, renewing our spiritual relationships, and rearming to reenter the world. Relevant worship is doing whatever it takes to be up on the mountain with Jesus. It's worship that really does make a difference. After Jesus' mountain experience, the Bible says that "angels came and began to minister to Him." Maybe when our worship becomes a mountaintop experience, we will start seeing the angels that God sends to minister to us or be entertained by us (Heb 13:2).

DISCUSSION QUESTIONS

1. When was the last significant spiritual change in your life?

2. How can the assembly be a retreat?

3. How can the assembly help us refocus on Jesus and our mission?

4. Is your assembly a time of renewal? Why or why not?

5. How can the assembly help us rearm and prepare to fight Satan?

6. What are some of the ways that we can spend time on the mountain with Jesus?

CHAPTER 17
Grab a Hand

I have always thought that it was a sign of spiritual maturity when a person spent more time praying for others than they did for themselves. Sometimes it's hard to tell the difference. It's like the college senior coed who prayed, "Lord, I'm not asking for myself, but please send my mother a son-in-law." Then there was little Raymond who returned home from Sunday school highly excited. He joyously told his mother, "The teacher prayed for me today." His mother said, "That's wonderful. What did she say?" He thought a second and said, "Lord we thank you for our food and Raymond."

There are close to a thousand prayers recorded in the Bible, but not many of them mention you and me. There is one notable exception. It should be exciting, yet humbling to know that Jesus, the Son of God, prayed specifically for us. It's not like there was nothing else to pray for, especially since it took place just hours before His ordeal on the cross. All the more reason for us to cherish His thoughtfulness and love as He remembered us in one of His last prayers on earth.

You may be wondering what Jesus' prayer in John 17 has to do with relevant worship. That should be obvious since He is praying about what He wants His followers to have as part of our lives. If it is part of our lives, then it's worship when we incorporate these things into our lives. Remember, these are things that were important enough for Jesus to pray for in the closing hours of His life. They are more than a "deathbed request" because they are from THE LORD, and they have eternal ramifications. They become essential elements in our worship to God, and because they are timeless, they are always relevant.

In verses 1-5, Jesus prayed about His fulfillment of God's plan. In verses 6-12, He prayed specifically for His apostles. In the remaining verses of chapter 17, He prayed for all of His disciples, both present and those to come, which as you know includes us. As I study this prayer I see four things that Jesus prayed for us to have. They are amazingly simple and practical, and must be made high-priority items for us, even if we have ignored them in the past.

The first thing He asked for us may be a shocker to you. He asked, ". . . that they may have My joy made full in themselves" (v. 13). His joy? He was about to face a terrible physical and emotional ordeal and death, and He wanted us to have His joy "made full" in all of us? How can joy be so important? Was this a different kind of joy than what most of us know?

This was not something new for Jesus to say. Earlier He had said, "These things I have spoken to you, that My joy may be in you, and that your joy may be made full" (John 15:11). He also had said, ". . . you . . . now have sorrow; but I will see you again, and your heart will rejoice, and no one takes your joy away from you." Then He promised, ". . . ask, and you will receive, that your joy may be made full" (John 16:22,24).

He was talking about a joy that they couldn't find from the world — a joy that the world couldn't understand. This is a joy based on faith in the heart and not a joy that was dependent on external circumstances. What was about to take place, His death and their temporary abandonment of Him, would not promote joy. But He wanted them to have His joy. His joy is full because it comes from an awareness of God's will being accomplished, seeing God's promises fulfilled; a joy that was sealed by an unsealed tomb.

If the joy that Jesus wants His disciples to have could transcend the horrors of the crucifixion, can't it transcend the disappointment of not having everything we want in our Christ-centered assemblies? That is a pretty big leap in application, but sometimes it's easier to see the big picture of a doctrinal concept than it is to see the smaller snapshots. Jesus died for us praying that we would be filled with His joy, and we have the nerve to sit in His assembly with folded arms grousing about some piddling point of preference? Jesus wanted us to have joy in spite of the world, not in spite of His Body, the church.

If we want relevant worship in our assemblies, we need to put joy back into our hearts. We need an unworldly joy that praises a resurrected Lord and holds Him up so that others can see Him in our lives. We need a joy that causes us to use our voices to "teach and admonish one another" rather than voice objections to one another. We can do it! Jesus prayed for it — doesn't God answer prayers?

Then Jesus prayed for us to have a life transformation because of His Word. He said, "I have given them Thy word; and the world has hated them, because they are not of the world, even as I am not of the world" (v. 14). When The Word is given and received, people are never the same again. His Word makes a difference in our lives. It changes our hearts, our priorities, and our acceptance by the world. He doesn't want us to be like the world, and when we are, we fail to fulfill His prayer for us.

This has endless application because it encompasses our whole life, which is appropriate since our whole life is worship to God. But let's just apply it to the Christian assembly. The Word of God is supposed to make such a difference in our lives that our assemblies should have nothing in them resembling worldly thinking or attitudes. Right? So when we say, "Yeah, that bunch of old legalists who run this church are never going to change anything," did we get that attitude from the Word or the world? From whom did we get the idea that "All you liberals want is change for change's sake. You don't care about our feelings at all"? How did our thinking about the assembly go from "What can I do to help you grow spiritually," to "Do something to make me feel good"? These things didn't come from the Word so they must have come from the world. If Jesus said, "I am not of the world," and we do and say things of the world in our assemblies, what does that say about us? How can we be people of "The Book" when "The Book" hasn't made us any less "of the world" than those without "The Book?"

Maybe we haven't been as committed to His Word as we thought we have. It can't be the fault of The Word. God said, ". . . My word . . . shall not return to Me empty" (Isa 55:11). So, if something is missing, it must be missing in us. Could it be that opinions, preferences, traditions, and our ideas have moved The Word off to the side? Are we as loyal to The Word, and making sure that we consistently apply it as we have always said we were? I suggest that we will have relevant worship in our assemblies when we start living the spirit of His Word and not just seeking doctrinal correctness. Let's not just have the right "acts" but the right attitudes. Jesus prayed for that, and God answers prayer!

The third thing that Jesus prays to His Father about for us really builds on the last request. Because we are transformed by His Word, and the world hates us, He petitions God to protect us. Again, we must see this in the context of what He is about to face. I would have been asking for protection from the Jews, the Romans, and the cross, not to mention the scourging, mocking, and nails. But if He had been protected from those things, you and I would have no hope. Thank God for that sacrifice of love and also for the love that caused Him to pray for our protection and ignore His own.

He asked God to ". . . keep them from the evil one. They are not of the world, even as I am not of the world. Sanctify them in the truth; thy word is truth" (John 17:15-17).

This is so rich with meaning and application that it is difficult not to expand on every word. In this short section of Jesus' prayer we see the prescription for godly living, and therefore, the cure for whatever ailments we may have in our assemblies. It's so simple, yet so complete. With God's help we must 1) stay away from Satan, 2) be like Jesus ("as I am"), and 3) be committed to His word, the truth. That is what Jesus prayed for, it's how God protects us, and it is always relevant worship.

We could pound each of these points into the worship assembly, but they are points that have been made several times already. Besides, there is a very relevant question that needs to be asked. Jesus prayed for God to protect us; did God answer His prayer?

Does Satan weasel his way into the church occasionally? Sure. Are there times when we act more like the world than like Jesus when we are meeting with the saints? Undeniably. Have there been instances when we have not been sanctified (set apart or committed) in the truth as we ought to have been? Certainly. Nevertheless, I believe that God's hand of protection has been over you and your church family in ways that we could never imagine. "God moves in a mysterious way" as He guards us from irreversible damage and destruction.

"God is faithful," Paul says, "who will not allow you to be tempted beyond what you are able, but with the temptation will provide the way of escape also, that you may be able to endure it" (1 Cor 10:13). This was promised to all Christians — the church. God will always provide a way of escape, a way to endure, and a way to stay faithful to Him. You'll never know how many times God protected your congregation from self-destruction. Have you ever wondered how you've stayed together with so much fussing and discontentment going on? He has been answering Jesus' prayer in your congregation ever since your first meeting. Why did some folks leave and some folks stay? Why do you have so many wonderful, warm memories? Why did you have that Bible teacher who did so much for you? Why did that elder suddenly resign? Why did you pick that preacher when so many applied for the job? Why — why — why? The questions are endless. God has been actively involved in protecting His church even when things seemed hopeless to you. He caused many people to grab your hand and lead you, comfort you, and support you. Then they took your hand and placed it in someone else's hand so you could do the same for them. That's why I believe that relevant worship is seeing the hand of God in our lives and our congregation's life. Truly relevant worship is reaching out with one hand and grabbing the hand of Jesus, while with our other hand we grab the hand of someone else and help them connect with Jesus too.

The purpose of the Christian assembly is for us to celebrate His joy, His Word, and His protection. As we meet together hand-to-hand and heart-to-heart, we commit ourselves to the primary goal of togetherness and the main focus of His prayer — unity. This is literally a dying plea from our Savior. Please notice the passion and intensity of Jesus' request to the Father.

> I do not ask in behalf of these alone, but for those also who believe in Me through their word; that they **may all be one**; even as Thou, Father, art in Me, and I in Thee,

that they also **may be in Us**; that the world may believe that Thou didst send Me.

And the glory which Thou hast given Me I have given to them; **that they may be one**, just as We are one; I in them, and Thou in Me, that they **may be perfected in unity**, that the world may know that Thou didst send Me, and didst love them, even as Thou didst love Me (vv. 20-23).

Isn't that incredible? Isn't it humbling? Isn't it touching? How it must hurt Him to see us squabble about preferences. How it must break His heart to see His followers, who He lived, prayed, and died for divide over opinions and let selfishness reign over submission. How can we be washed by His blood and not moved by His tears?

This passage is the Magna Carta of unity. It speaks to the very soul of what we are and to whom we belong. All the usual words that could be used to describe how important this is are inadequate. Words like essential, foundational, cardinal, and primary are too overused to really impress on our minds how all-inclusive this is. I can't do it justice in a few paragraphs of prose, but I would like to apply His plea for unity to the widespread turmoil about the assembly that seems to be sweeping across the brotherhood. After all, it is when we are together that unity is practiced. The rest of the time it's just theory.

The worship assembly is God's lighthouse of unity. Congregations that are fussing, fuming, and fragmenting over trying to please everyone in the assembly are lighthouses with burned-out lights. We have lighthouses all across the country that aren't saving people from the rocky shores or pointing anyone in the right direction. They look quaint and are interesting to visit, but they don't function as intended. They are manned by caretakers instead of care-givers.

Jesus prayed for unity so that our collective light would shine with the glory of God in a dark world of sin and dis-

209

unity. He didn't pray for us to have unanimity, because it's impossible to have absolute agreement in opinions. He didn't pray for us to have uniformity, because we are all different parts of the Body. (See 1 Cor 12:12-27.) He didn't pray for us to be a union, like a social club, or a civic or political organization. He prayed for a spiritual unity that must be preeminent, progressive, and promotable. If this isn't seen in the assembly, where can it be seen?

Jesus prayed for our unity to be a **Preeminent Unity**. This is speaking to the level of importance that He wants unity to have in our lives. We know it must be a high priority because He wants us to have unity that is just like what He and the Father have. He said, "as Thou, Father, art in Me, and I in Thee," and again, "that they may be one as we are one." Can you think of a higher, more complete unity than what the Father and the Son have? They have a unity that goes beyond comprehension. We call it the doctrine of the trinity. The Father, Son, and Holy Spirit are totally united, yet still three distinct beings. We are to strive for that kind of closeness.

Several times I have pointed out that part of the reason why we have problems in the assembly is due to the preeminence we have given it. The assembly was never intended to be the focus of our religion, the litmus test of our faithfulness, and the sole (soul) provider of our spiritual nutrition. It is one of the tools given to us by God to be used by us for spiritual growth. What is and must be preeminent, however, is unity! If we would put half the energy into unifying our congregation as we do in expressing our dissatisfaction, we'd be well on our way to being what Jesus prayed for us to be. Brethren, we need to stop making mountains out of molehills and stop seeing the mountains as molehills. Unity in Christ is a mountain! This is not some take-it-or-leave-it gray area where we each have our own preference. Jesus prayed that we be one as He and the Father were one, and did you notice the next phrase? He added, "**. . . that they also may be in Us.**" Have we somehow missed that throughout the years? Am I misunderstanding Him or is He not saying that if we aren't one with each other we may not be one with Him and the Father?

Please think of that the next time you start thinking, "Wouldn't it be great to just start a new church? A church with no traditions to protect and no set-in-their-ways brethren to keep happy? Wouldn't it be great to do only new, snappy songs, have drama, singing groups, more spontaneity, and a relaxed, informal atmosphere? Yeah, we could do that and call it outreach, or church planting, or, or, or . . . relevant worship!"

We all know what we would like to see in the assembly. I would like to see several new things in the assembly. I don't need it, but I'd like to see it, **but not at the expense of hurting the Body of Christ!** There should be no greater preference that any of us have than unity in Christ. If we can't make it a high-priority item for one or two hours a week, when can we? When did Jesus expect us to have this oneness like He and the Father had if it's not when we are together — together in His name?

The unity Jesus prayed for must also be a **Progressive Unity**. That is not referring to an ideological slant, but rather a literal growing, improving, progressing unity. It's seen in the words "that they may be one." God has empowered us to have unity. The potential is there, but we, with His help, have to make it happen. Permission and power have been given; discipleship means we accepted the challenge.

This progressive unity is also seen in Jesus' request "that they may be perfected in unity." We all know that in biblical usage "perfected" means complete or whole. He doesn't want us to just "sort of" work at unity, He wants us to commit to the whole process, do whatever it takes, and never stop until we are "perfected in unity."

Man may judge successful churches in terms of large attendance and mega-bucks contributions, but Jesus says that no church is whole or complete until it has unity. How are you progressing in unity? It is far more important than defending traditions or instituting new ideas. Unity can't be put on the shelf for a few years and then retrieved after you've gotten what you wanted.

Jesus also made it clear that this unity was a **Promotable Unity**. He wants us to have unity so "that the world may believe that Thou didst send Me." The second time He mentioned this He added, "that the world may know" that God sent Him and that He loves them. Unity is God's outreach program. He said that our unity will cause the unchurched to hear, believe, and know the Gospel message, that God sent Jesus to save us. Our unity will create faith and help others to see the love of God. Jesus said that would happen. If it hasn't, then maybe we don't have the kind of unity we think we do.

Jesus had already told His disciples that the world would know they were His disciples if they loved one another (John 13:35). Unity is love in action. It is the reason why the early church grew so fast. Remember the first days of the Jerusalem church? The Bible tells us, "And day by day continuing with one mind in the temple, and breaking bread from house to house, they were taking their meals together with gladness and sincerity of heart, praising God, and having favor with all the people. And the Lord was adding to their number day by day those who were being saved" (Acts 2:46-47).

Take a pencil and underline everything in that short passage that touches unity. Is it any wonder that folks were flocking to the church in those days? People were literally on the outside looking in and saying "I want some of that!" That is what unity will do for us. It will help us draw closer to God, Jesus, one another, and cause the people in the community to perk up and see what a difference love can make. They will see real relevant worship and say, "I want some of that!"

Unity is more than mere peaceful coexistence. That is part of it, as Paul said, "If possible, so far as it depends on you, be at peace with all men" (Rom 12:18). He was referring there to living in peace with the world. In the great unity passage, Ephesians 4, Paul said for us to be "diligent to preserve the unity of the Spirit in the bond of peace" (v. 3). Our unity is in the Spirit. It is a spiritual unity that transcends all human barriers or differences, but we must be diligent to make it happen. He then lists the seven things that unite us. They are simple and easy to understand. Our unity consists of one body, one Spirit, and one hope, which says to me that we are one family. Then we have one Lord, one faith, and one baptism, which says to me that we all have the same relationship with Jesus. The last is "one God and Father of all," which simply means that we have the same Head of the family.

It's easy to look at these seven things and say, "Yeah, we have unity because we agree on all seven of these things." But, doctrinal unity is not necessarily Christlike unity. Unity must be more than intellectual agreement or religious affiliation. The real key to unity is found in the attitude we have as we commit to unity. Paul begged us to "walk in a manner worthy of the calling" to which we have been called. This means that we approach the preservation of unity with "all humility and gentleness, with patience, showing forbearance to one another in love" (v. 2).

In the context of maintaining unity, aren't these incredible concepts for Paul to be calling for from us? All of these impact how we treat each other. It would seem that is the real challenge of unity — to treat each other in a Christlike manner. When it comes to disagreements over the assembly, are you sensitive, unselfish, considerate, kind, and forgiving? These are the attitudes we take with us to congregational meetings, elders meetings, ministry meetings, and one-on-one meetings. When Christians have this kind of an attitude, unity reigns supreme, brethren grow closer, God is worshiped, and outsiders "want some of that."

DISCUSSION QUESTIONS

1. How would the joy of Christ make us look at the assembly differently?

2. Are most criticisms of the assembly from members based on the Word or the world?

3. Did God answer Jesus' prayer to protect us? How?

4. How does Satan occasionally weasel his way into our assemblies?

5. Jesus prayed for our unity. What are we doing to help fulfill that request?

6. How important is unity to you? What are you willing to sacrifice for it?

CHAPTER 18
Pick Up a Cross

In Ralph Martin's insightful little book, *Worship in the Early Church*, he makes an interesting point:

> The thought that the Church at worship is an accidental convergence in one place of a number of isolated individuals who practice, in hermetically sealed compartments, their own private devotional exercises, is foreign to the New Testament picture.[21]

The assembly is a togetherness event. As we climb the mountain with Jesus, we grab the hands of others who sometimes lead us and are sometimes led by us. It's being together in Christ and helping one another grow that makes the assembly such a powerful experience. If the assembly isn't the place to be unselfish, where is the place?

Jesus said, "If anyone wishes to come after Me, let him deny himself, and take up his cross, and follow Me" (Matt

16:24). We can't say that we've picked up our cross and followed Jesus if we haven't denied ourselves. Again, if we don't do these things in the assembly of the saints, when and where do we do them? Can you imagine what a difference it would make in your assembly if everyone denied self, picked up a cross, and followed Jesus? That is what Jesus wants. We deny self, we don't get what we want! We pick up a cross, we don't get cross and picky! We follow Jesus and not the crowd with its petty preferences. It may very well be that Satan's greatest success is getting people to believe that they should go to the assembly to get rather than give.

What style of worship assembly do you like? Do you like it because of what it does for you or because of what it gives to others? In my first book about worship and the assembly (*Spilt Grape Juice*), a good part of the book was dedicated to describing what should happen in the Christian assembly. According to the New Testament, there were three things that the early Christians were supposed to make sure happened when they got together. They met to encourage one another, to edify one another, and to equip one another. (See Heb 10:24-25; 1 Cor 14:26; Eph 4:12-16.) There are plenty of Scriptures that could and should be studied so that we can understand how important these three activities are, but we may miss the most obvious point. These are all things that we do for others and not things we do for ourselves. We meet to encourage, to edify, and to equip others, and we will in turn be encouraged, edified, and equipped by them, but it's what we need to do for others that motivates us to not miss the assembly.

Picking up a cross and following Jesus is real worship. If our assembly is going to be an extension of that worship, we'd better not park our cross in the foyer when we get there. Unfortunately that happens all too often. For some reason many folks believe that the assembly is where you talk about the cross, but carrying it is something you do afterwards. It is the same way with all of the "one another"

216

passages in the New Testament. We study them in Bible class, preach about them in the assembly, and read about them in our church bulletin, but we don't see how they are relevant or applicable in the assembly. Again, if we don't apply these to the assembly, when Christians are together, when do we apply them?

When do you do these in your assembly?

Love one another – John 13:34

Encourage one another – Heb 10:25

Stimulate one another to love and good deeds – Heb 10:24

Bear with one another – Col 3:13

Forgive one another – Col 3:13

Teach and admonish one another – Col 3:16

Be kind to one another – Eph 4:32

Confess your sins to one another – James 5:16

Pray for one another – James 5:16

Greet one another with a holy kiss – Rom 16:16

Be subject to one another – Ephs 5:21

Bear one another's burdens – Gal 6:2

Pursue the things which make for peace and the building up of one another – Rom 16:19

Be devoted to one another in brotherly love – Rom 12:10

Give preference to one another in honor – Rom 12:10

Be of the same mind toward one another – Rom 12:16

Build up one another – 1 Thess 5:11

Seek after that which is good for one another – 1 Thess 5:15

Have fellowship with one another – 1 John 1:7

Speak to one another in psalms and hymns – Eph 5:19

Even in the best of congregations, these are reduced to foyer activities and post-closing prayer events. These are the things we meet to do, but in our rush to maintain our traditional way of "doing worship," we kicked them out of the assembly. It shouldn't surprise anyone that these attitudes are not present, then, to help overcome assembly problems. All of these wonderful "one another" passages, and there are many more, make it clear that we come together to give — to do for others, and not to have others push all of our preference buttons to make us feel good. We can't pick up our cross without picking up all of our "one another" responsibilities. When the assembly becomes a "one another" activity again, it will then be part of what relevant worship is all about.

In the midst of all the conflict over assembly styles, we sometimes forget that carrying a cross means loving one another — in spite of our differences. We can't afford to allow love to slip to a less than preeminent place in our lives. It is why Jesus died, it is what God wants from us, and it is the only thing that will abide. John tells us that it is impossible to love God and not love one another, because we love God by loving one another. Forget that junk about horizontal and vertical love or worship. Satan loves it when we create religious descriptions that don't follow Bible teachings. The way to know that we love God, abide in God, have Jesus as our brother and advocate before God, and that we are keeping His commandments is to love one another. (See 1 John 4:7-21.) It's that simple and that essential! We can't minimize brotherly love or cheapen it by letting assembly preferences become more important.

Paul described the attributes of love in 1 Corinthians 13 and sometimes we apply them to everything but when Christians are together. It's great wedding material and wonderful memory work for a Bible class, but expecting it in the worship assembly . . . ? If not there, then where? Can you think of a better place for patience, kindness, unselfishness, humility, sensible behavior, calmness, forgiveness, righteousness, endurance, faith, hope, and unfailing love?

You want new songs, an upbeat tempo to everything, and in general, a contemporary flavor to your worship assembly. Or maybe you want the stability of predictability. You're comfortable with the traditional way things are done, with a never-changing schedule and songs you've sung since you were a kid. Do you value comfort? Maybe it's important to you that the assembly be outreach oriented? Could it be that you like . . . well, no matter what you like, love is and always will be "the greatest of these." We must not sacrifice love on the altar of "I like" or "I want." The cross we choose to carry is a cross of love, and it's our will (deny self) that gets sacrificed. Please remember that when you start promoting or defending against changes in the assembly. If love isn't there, what difference does it make what happens in the assembly? If, however, love is dominant in our assembly . . . well, what difference does it make what happens in the assembly, when you've got love for one another!

It is easy to forget how important brotherly love is in the grand scheme of things. We get so busy doing spiritual things that we sometimes forget to be spiritual. Love is not just a part of our religion, it is our religion. God is love, remember. (See 1 John 4:8.) Love is more than an element, a focal point, or a major doctrine. It's being like God! The preeminence of love in our faith was brought home to me by a passage I was preaching on in 1 Peter. What was most amazing about it was that it wasn't the usual big religious terms that made me sit up and recognize this point, but rather two simple, almost unnoticed words. Peter is wrapping up his letter and he declares, "The end of all things is at hand; therefore, be of sound judgment and sober spirit for the purpose of prayer" (1 Pet 4:7).

This is great preaching material; the end — sound judgment — sober spirit — prayer! This is important STUFF! But then Peter said, "Above all." Now "above all" is a phrase that is used to indicate that what follows is more important than everything thus far. Can this really be more important than sound judgment, sober spirit, and prayer? What could possibly be that important? "Above all, keep fervent in your love for one another, because love covers a multitude of sins" (1 Pet 4:8).

Love is the top priority. Peter wants us to understand that we must fervently work at loving one another, more than we work at anything else, because it does so much. Do you think that brethren are wrong because they give so much emphasis to tradition? Do you think that those folks who seem to always want change are "treading on dangerous ground" biblically? Whatever the problem is that you think others have, "love covers a multitude of sins" — yours, mine, and ours! Love gives us the chance to be on the cross and be in the forgiveness business! That is far more important than any style preferences we may have, even if our motivation for the preference is unselfish. It's what people do who have chosen to pick up a cross and follow Jesus. It's also what true relevant worship is all about.

DISCUSSION QUESTIONS

1. What style of worship assembly do you like best? Why?

2. What does picking up a cross have to do with how we view the assembly?

3. Review the "one another" passages and discuss how these could be accomplished in the assembly.

4. If love dominates your assembly, what difference does it make what kind of style you have?

5. How does love cover "a multitude of sins" in the asssembly?

CHAPTER 19
Developing a Relevant
Worship Assembly

They were women of the night — prostitutes, and for some reason they were living together. Maybe it was to help each other deliver the babies that each one was about to have. They both gave birth to healthy babies, but one night one of the new mothers rolled over on top of her baby and accidently crushed it to death. She compounded this terrible disaster by switching her dead baby with the other mother's live baby, unbelievably thinking that she wouldn't notice. She did, and now they were standing before the wise King Solomon, each one declaring that the living child was hers.

Solomon asked for a sword to be brought and for the living child to be cut in two. Each mother was to receive one half. Before the sword could fall, one of the mothers quickly said, "Oh, my Lord, give her the living child, and by no means kill him." The other woman argued, "He shall be neither mine nor yours; divide him!"

It was obvious to all who the real mother was, and Solomon ordered the child to be given to her. She was the one who was willing to lose the child as long as he could be kept alive. She was willing to sacrifice her right to be a mother for the sake of the child. (See 1 Kgs 3:16-28.).

While the story is told to show the wisdom of Solomon, it is a beautiful example of unselfish love. This story is analogous to the church today. The church is the Body of Christ, God's Son, and some are ready to let the sword fall if they can't get what they want. If it were over matters of doctrinal purity and fighting the good fight of faith, maybe the Sword of the Spirit would need to fall. But brethren aren't fighting mad over essentials but over opinions and preferences. We need unselfish love that says, "Let's do it your way, only don't let any harm come to the Body." It wasn't easy for that mother long ago and it won't be easy for us today, but it's what love does. And isn't that what Jesus did?

On many occasions when I have been part of a discussion on worship and the assembly, I have made the comment that every Christian should read Romans 14 and 15 at least once a week. These great passages, along with 1 Corinthians 8, need to be studied regularly by us because they lay out the principles by which Christians are to resolve disagreements, especially in the area of opinions. I wish we had the space to do it here, but the basic principle is that the stronger, more spiritually mature Christian is to sacrifice his or her rights and liberty for the sake of the weaker, or less mature brother. The mature know better what we have liberty to do, but Paul said that "Knowledge makes arrogant, but love edifies," and the mature are committed to not doing anything that would cause a weaker brother to stumble. (See 1 Cor 8:1,9,13.)

Mature Christians give up their rights for the sake of the immature brethren who haven't yet come to a full understanding of the freedom they have in Christ. In talking about eating certain food Paul said, "If food causes my brother to stumble, I will never eat meat again, that I might not cause my brother to stumble" (1 Cor 8:13). Later he said, "Do not destroy with your food him for whom Christ died. Therefore, do not let what is for you a good thing be spoken of as evil" (Rom 14:15-16). Then he added, "Do not tear down the work of God for the sake of food" (Rom 14:20).

An interesting and convicting activity is to apply these same verses to our preferences. What do you want in your assembly? Do you want a snappy, fast-paced schedule, with contemporary songs, variety in the communion, and a really upbeat sermon? Do you want things to return to "the good old days" with old standard songs and a predictable format? Neither of these styles is wrong, unless you believe they come from the Bible, and anyone who does something different is in error. They are both preferences! As long as we maintain scriptural accuracy, we have liberty to do whatever we like or whatever is expedient. We need to make sure that what we like can pass the biblical Maturity Test.

For example, of all the things that brethren have sharply disagreed about in the assembly, singing and things related to singing seem to be at the top of the list. I guess because music really touches the heart, brethren get very emotional about what they like and don't like. So they disagree about types of songs, the beat of songs, the number of songs, the leading of songs, and the use of praise teams, worship leaders, solos, and choruses. If any one of these things is more important to you than your brother in Christ, you've already failed the Maturity Test. Now use the passages mentioned above and replace the word "food" with whatever it is you prefer.

If _____ causes my brother to stumble, I will never _____ again, that I might not cause my brother to stumble.

Do not destroy with your _____ him for whom
Christ died.

Do not tear down the work of God for the sake of
_____.

This has nothing to do with whether or not your idea or
preference is good or bad. It simply means that we operate
from a spirit of love, unselfishness, and humility. Your idea
or preference may just be what your congregation needs,
but it must be carefully, considerately, and patiently discussed, examined, and prayed about long before it's introduced.

The problem with applying all these wonderful principles about the stronger and weaker brother is that no one
can agree on who's who. For some reason, when it comes
to the assembly, the seventy-year-old brother, who has
been a Christian for over fifty years, wants to be considered as the weaker brother by the Boomers and Busters so
they will do things his way. And, oddly enough, those
Christians who have grown so much, and been enlightened
about liberty in Christ, want the older, more mature
brethren to "not put an obstacle or a stumbling block in a
brother's way," by refusing to change. Are there any
stronger brethren left, or have we all regressed into weaker
brothers? Who gives in to whom?

If I understand these passages, every Christian is "bend-
ing over backwards" to give in to one another. It's because
of Christ that we "submit to one another," and that's
reason enough. Can you imagine what it would be like at a
church business meeting for brethren to insist that we do
what the other brother prefers, and he refuses because he
wants to be submissive and let his brother have what he
wants? Wow! Won't that be a novel discussion? It could
even make business meetings fun again.

The point should be obvious by now. Whatever you
want to see happen in your congregation's assembly must

be subordinated to the development of the mind of Christ in every member. Only when churches have a Christlike spirit can they make unselfish decisions to change things for the cause of Christ and not personal preferences. It's only when there is a servant spirit that brethren can restudy the subject of worship and see that God has given us great leeway in using the assembly as a tool for spiritual growth, and we can change to do those things that make it as productive as possible in order to carry out the mission He has given us.

So, even with a quarter-century of study and experience in this subject, it's with sincere humility that I offer the following suggestions:

1. Decide it's time to do something — anything — that will move your congregation into a closer relationship with God, each other, and closer to the reality of carrying out His mission. I have often said, "Do something, even if it's wrong." I'm not talking about violating Scripture and anything connected with being Christlike, but I am saying don't be afraid to risk failure! Our job is to try! God said He would take care of the winning and the success, if it's His will. But many congregations are going to have to give an account to God for allowing His church to dwell in a rut. There is nothing admirable or Christlike about apathy, indifference, laziness, intolerance, maintaining the status quo, or allowing His church to slowly decline through ignorance or lack of involvement in His mission. Is it time to wake up, shake up, and get up and start growing at your church? It begins with the leaders, and through active shepherding it spreads to every member.

2. Spend a lot of time in prayer and study. You know that, but this must be more than personal prayer and study. There must be a great deal of togetherness praying and studying. Plan a three month congregational time of prayer and study on the topic "What does God want this church to be?" Have every adult Bible class study and pray about

this, and have the preacher present a series of sermons on it too. Have special prayer meetings, congregational fasting, bring in resource people, have congregational and leadership seminars. Whenever and wherever you can, pray. You've heard all your life that "the family that prays together stays together." It is also true for church families. Praying together bonds members. It takes everything to a higher spiritual level where love dominates and personal preferences are diminished. It gives purpose, drive, and a sense of the presence of God.

This is simple soil preparation. If you don't develop a spiritual environment there won't be a desire for spiritual growth. Too often, we've dropped changes on brethren who were about as ready for change as a child is for a vaccination. Prayer is communication with God. Bible study is God communicating with us. Doing these things together, with a purpose, builds unity and expectancy. Besides, if you can't get people excited with a greater emphasis on prayer, study, and togetherness, you have your answer to #1.

3. Now that you've turned up the spiritual heat, it's time to study worship. Don't purchase any books yet. (I'm sure my publisher will forgive me.) Use the only book that counts, the Word of God. Allow four to six weeks for a congregational study of what the Bible has to say about worship and the assembly. Emphasize your reliance on and commitment to the Word. Highlight the Restoration plea over and over again. IT'S NOT DEAD OR IRRELEVANT! Pray before, during, and after each class.

Challenge every member to attempt total objectivity. Ask them to imagine that they knew nothing about worship, going to church, what the assembly is or ever has been, and also ask them not to have any preconceived ideas about what they will learn. It is impossible to do this completely, but the idea is to have them start looking at the New Testament with a fresh perspective.

Ask for every member to have a Christlike spirit about the study too. Pray about removing pride, smugness, divisiveness, hidden agendas, and anything that Satan could use to hinder your study. The study is not a witch hunt, a tradition bashing, or an opportunity to impress everyone with your progressiveness. Ask for humility, submissiveness, love, and a willingness to make this a spiritual adventure into real New Testament Christianity.

I would develop a study sheet that would be simple and merely provide direction and encourage discussion. It would be something like this:

A CONGREGATIONAL STUDY OF WORSHIP AND THE ASSEMBLY IN THE NEW TESTAMENT

Scriptures:	What?	Why?	When?	Us?
John 4:19-24				
Romans 12:1-3				
Hebrews 12:28				
Hebrews 13:15-16				
Acts 2:41-47				
Acts 20:1-11				
1 Corinthians 10–14				
Ephesians 4:1-16				
Hebrews 10:23-25				
James 2:1-13				
Colossians 3:12-17				
1 Timothy 4:13				
1 Timothy 4:1-4				
1 Timothy 2:8				
Romans 16:16				
1 Corinthians 16:1-2				

These are just some of the passages you can use. Add others, or arrange them any way you like. The WHAT column is to list and describe what they did. For some of these passages, like Acts 2 or 1 Corinthians 10-14, you will need a lot of space. The WHY column is to simply ask and answer the question, why did they do this? The WHEN column is the easiest because most of these passages don't tell you when they did these things, but it isn't hard to speculate.

Anytime there is dissension or strong disagreements, stop and pray. The spirit is more important than the conclusions! When the study is over, everyone should know that this is what we have from God about worship and the assembly. Everything else we have or do comes from man. That doesn't mean that it's good or bad, it just means that we have freedom to do whatever is necessary to carry out the will of God. Now the real question is "Do we know what the will of God is for us?"

4. Develop a congregational vision. With a lot of prayer and congregational communication, put together a group that is a cross section of all the congregation to meet with the leadership and develop a vision for the church. This is not the developing of a mission. In my opinion, our mission is clearly spelled out in Scripture. The Great Commission is our mission. Specifically, Paul said, ". . . the mystery which for ages has been hidden in God, who created all things; in order that the manifold wisdom of God might now be made known through the church to the rulers and the authorities in the heavenly places. This was according to His eternal purpose which He carried out in Christ Jesus our Lord" (Eph 3:9-11). To carry out this great mission we must be unified in love and growing in Christ. (See Eph 4:11-16.) This is the mission of every congregation.

A church vision is a picture of what God wants this particular congregation to be. How can this church, using its talents, gifts, and spiritual maturity, and taking into account the age, diversity, demographics, and potential growth or changes, carry out the mission of God? Why did God put us here?

Get plenty of input from every member. Use surveys, small discussion groups, and consider hiring the services of an objective outside organization that can help you understand who you are, what you have, and what you can do. I know firsthand that an outside expert can say the exact same things that the preacher or elders have been saying, but he is heard and received because there is no reason to question his motives.

This is not a book about church growth, but about worship and the assembly. But, one of the things you should discover is the level of satisfaction or dissatisfaction you have in your congregation about the assembly. And one of the major conclusions you may reach when you decide what God wants you to be will be to change the style of your assembly. This stage requires even more prayer and congregational communication.

The congregation must accept and have ownership of the committee's/leadership's vision for the church. Leaders have a primary responsibility to provide direction for the church, but they must not "lord it over" the sheep. It must be prayerfully sold! Once the congregation has accepted the vision, and they know what they want to be, it will then be easier to accept the changes necessary to accomplish that vision.

5. Decide how you will use the assembly as a tool to accomplish your God-given vision. What are the goals? Members must be edified and encouraged through the assembly. That's required and must not be omitted. But what about your other goals, like building excitement, appealing and holding younger Christians, making brethren excited about inviting unchurched friends, and possibly reaching out to those folks when they attend? What style of assembly will this require? Is everyone in agreement on these objectives? Have the needs and concerns of every member been completely dealt with? Have you been honest? Can you accept it if most of the congregation

would like to see new people attend and young folks not leave, but they don't want to change anything to make that happen?

One worship committee that I was a member of had extensive discussions with older, more conservative members about changes in the assembly. To my surprise, it wasn't so much the changes that concerned them but the way in which they were introduced. Three key points quickly surfaced. First, communicate all changes well in advance of instituting them. Second, show that they have been thoroughly examined, researched, and well thought through. Last, make it clear that the elders want it and support it. All three of these elements are essential and should be followed before any change is made. These are easy things to do to help comfort those who may be seriously disturbed by new things.

With all other considerations taken care of, what are you going to do with your assembly? It belongs to Jesus, but He put the tool in your hands and said use it. Ralph P. Martin, in his book *Worship in the Early Church*, makes the point, ". . . there is, of course, no place in the New Testament which clearly states that the Church had any set order of service, and very little information is supplied to us about the outward forms which were in use."[22] Actually, if you go back to your filled-out study sheet about worship and the assembly, you'll see that they did a lot of things when they came together. There are a lot of God-given tools available and the possible combinations are endless.

At this point, we must remember two essential truths about congregational growth and the changes required to bring it about. First, congregational morale isn't just something, it's everything. If a church doesn't have the right spirit of love for one another, unity, and a deep desire to DO God's will, all the planning and changing in the world will do nothing but provide more grist for the murmuring mill. The single most important need in every church is for the mind of Christ to be developed in every member. Failure to take the time to prepare the soil will result in a failed crop. Be patient. Build a close family. Give God plenty of time to do His work in the hearts of every member.

The second truth that must rule every decision is, **it is never wrong to do anything purely for the sake of church unity**. I am not referring to doctrinal absolutes, but styles, preferences, opinions, and changes. There is no need to apologize or feel like a failure because for the sake of unity, you didn't change something. This does not mean that you follow the loud voices of a small minority. A few are going to stay "bent out of shape" no matter what you do, and there will always be folks church hopping because they didn't get their way. I am referring to that 75% to 85% core in your church, who are not extremists, but just want to do what is best for the cause of Christ.

If you've prepared the soil, determined a direction, and that core membership is behind it, press on! But, make sure you are sensitive, well informed about the membership, and doing what they really understand and agree must be done. Don't force something that destroys unity and hurts the love that is supposed to identify you as belonging to Jesus.

6. Do what works best, not what has always been done. For example, how much time do you want your church family to be together on Sunday? What is the best way to use that time? Traditionally we have a Bible class, a worship assembly, and an evening assembly. Is that the best way to use three hours of togetherness on Sunday? What is the best way to make sure that you break bread together? You've got three hours to do three things: break the bread of sharing Jesus, break the bread of communion, and break the bread of a shared meal. Could that be done with everyone making only one trip to the building? Can they be mixed together and spread out over a three-hour period?

How about being together for an hour and a half on Sunday and an hour and a half some other time during the week? Both time and scheduling are expediencies.

How can you have the best, most uplifting singing possible? How can the communion be made more meaningful and more a sharing event? How can we make our prayer time more of a sharing event, besides all of us bowing our heads at the same time? Can we share prayer needs, confess faults, voice spiritual successes and blessings, and really express love for one another before we pray about it? How can we use our time to build unity and closeness? What is the best way to share the Bread of Life and help one another know Jesus better? Where else in modern times do we depend on a thirty-minute lecture to give life-changing information? We must teach and preach to one another, but that does not limit the avenues of communication techniques we can use. Can we use audio-visual devices to teach one another about Jesus, and maybe provide mental pictures that will help it to last? How can we teach and encourage one another through the use of short skits, monologues, or Biblical reenactments? Jesus used visuals and stories to illustrate His lessons. In Acts 21:10-11, a prophet named Agabus took Paul's belts and used them to tie up his own hands and feet. He did this to show Paul and all those present what the Jews would do to Paul if he went back to Jerusalem. I'd call that pretty dramatic, wouldn't you?

The list of questions that you need to ask and answer is as long as you want it to be. Ideally, if you have the freedom to do it, the answers should be based on what glorifies God and is the best way to carry out your vision. Only your church can answer these questions. You don't have to be like any other church and you don't have to listen to anyone else's suggestions about what you should do — including mine. The real question is not "To change or not to change," or should we have a contemporary or traditional worship assembly or both, but rather how can we best glorify God. Whatever you do, please put *koinonia* back into your togetherness times, and above all else, don't let Satan win!

DISCUSSION QUESTIONS

1. What would you be willing to sacrifice to protect the Body of Christ (the church)?

2. Look at the Maturity Test and place your assembly preferences in the blanks.

3. Why is it so hard to determine who the weaker or stronger brother is with today's assembly issues?

4. Why is developing the mind of Christ far more important than any assembly preference?

5. Discuss each of the suggestions for developing a relevant assembly.

CONCLUSION
Pretty or Crumby

A loaf of homemade bread is beautiful to see, but even better to smell. Of course the best way to experience bread is to taste it. If a loaf of bread is never broken and eaten, it becomes stale, hard, and unappetizing. It may still look pretty, but that's just because the "upper crust" looks so good. Inside it's petrified. Any analogies come to mind yet?

When Christians come together Jesus wants some bread to be broken. We should leave our assemblies with crumbs covering our laps and the floor of wherever we met. The intent is not to fill our stomachs, though there's nothing wrong with that, but to fill our hearts with the love of one another and with the love of God. Bread breaking is sharing, not performing; it's giving, not getting; and it's bonding, not dividing. It's simple, biblical, and effective. That is why God told us to do it, and the way the New Testament Christians did it. It is also part of the reason why others were attracted to them and "the Lord was adding to their number day by day."

We've spent too many years looking pretty as a church and not breaking the bread of real New Testament Christianity. It's time to start causing some crumbs to appear in our assembly! If we're going to have true *koinonia* we are going to have some crumbs, because we will be breaking a lot of bread. Why have buildings and furniture that aren't conducive to bread breaking? Why wear clothes that you don't want to get crumbs on? Why call yourself a New Testament church when you don't even follow its pattern by breaking bread when you assemble?

Breaking the Bread of Life (Jesus), the bread of communion, and the bread of fellowship (including meals) means we are following the example of the church in Jerusalem (Acts 2), the church in Troas (Acts 20), and the church in Corinth (1 Corinthians 10-14). From other passages of Scripture we can see that this bread breaking included other things like singing, praying, sharing material wealth, greeting, equipping, encouraging, and loads of "one another" activities. When we fail to follow this New Testament pattern, bread goes unbroken and left to get stale and worthless.

The only viable solution to the present-day assembly battleground is emphasizing and developing the mind of Christ in every member through genuine, loving relationship building. When brethren love each other and are driven by a desire to help one another and thereby worship God through obedience to His commands, assembly styles become irrelevant, spiritual growth can't be stopped, and the unchurched are attracted.

The simple breaking of bread that was the focal point of New Testament togetherness is so far removed from either the formalism of our traditional assemblies or the slick, professional performances of some contemporary assemblies. Whether either of these is right or wrong, good or bad, better or best, depends on the hearts of the participants, but somehow we need to get back that simple togetherness, where brethren shared, interacted, encouraged, and loved one another.

For this to happen we will have to rethink our traditional understanding of worship. When brethren learn that worship is our life, the pressure and focus will be taken from the assembly and placed on consistent Christlike living. The assembly can then become the uplifting celebration of salvation, unity, and unselfishness that it was intended to be. The focus can return to being on Jesus our King as we stop trying to have a king like all the nations (religions) surrounding us.

We must stay committed to our primary goal of worshiping God by being living sacrifices, offered in loving obedience to Him. That is the only way to keep our wants and preferences in check. We don't have to "get what we want" because we are driven to give Him what He wants.

King David woke up one morning and was overwhelmed with gratitude for God. God had protected him and led him through the many attempts by Saul to destroy him. He had blessed his family and followers. God was there in the difficult years of his early rule as King when half the nation refused to pledge allegiance to him as their new leader. And now, with the nation unified and most of his enemies defeated, David wanted to do something for God. His idea? Build a temple for God.

It seemed like a great idea. In 2 Samuel 7:2-3 David told the prophet Nathan about his plan, and Nathan essentially said, "Go for it!" Later, however, when Nathan talked to God about it, God didn't think it was such a great idea. The bottom line was that David was told "No, you can't do that." While God did make a covenant with David and promise him that his son would build the House of God, David still had to cope with not getting what he wanted (vv. 5-17).

David didn't stomp off mad, and he didn't grumble to his friends about how his good idea was rejected. Instead he prayed, and his prayer in 2 Samuel 7:18-29 is a beautiful portrait of submission that is completely free from any hint of resentment. What we see is **humility** as he asks "Who am I . . ." and "what more can David say to Thee?" He adds, "For the sake of Thy word, and according to Thine own heart, Thou hast done all this greatness to let thy servant know" (vv. 18-21).

This is followed by **praise** for God for all the "awesome things" He has done for David and His people (vv. 22-24). He concludes his prayer with a **recommitment** to serving God, accepting His decisions, and magnifying His name (vv. 25-29).

It's simple, it's biblical, and it works, but it only works when our hearts are honest and open before God. When you don't get your way, reject resentment by humbly praising God and by recommitting yourself to accepting His will. That is what God wants.

Many congregations will continue to stay in turmoil about assembly styles. Members will continue to quietly slip out the back door and find a new church that "better meets their needs." Some churches will have splits as some decide it is easier to start a new church than get the older one to change. It will not be an act of bringing glory to God, but a tribute to intolerance and misplaced priorities. Some will make serious changes out of the conviction that God's will can't be done in an atmosphere of belligerence. While that is not always true, each of us must do what we feel is best for the spiritual welfare of the Lord's church, our families, our own peace of mind, and to honestly respond to what we feel God's will is for us.

Don't let pride and selfishness rule! Are you honestly grieving over your church's failure to reach out to the surrounding community with the Gospel? Are you truly worried about the loss of future generations, and maybe your own children? Is it really your conscience that is driving you to want change or to fight change? Only you can answer those heart-level questions, but let me add one more. How much time have you spent breaking bread with brethren who disagree with you? I'm talking about all three kinds of bread breaking. Have you broken the Bread of Life together? Have you met at the foot of the cross and broken the bread of remembrance, love, self-examination, and recommitment? Have you shared a dinner table that was loaded with lovingly prepared food and broken the bread of fellowship?

I am totally convinced that when brethren break bread they won't break hearts, and when hearts become bonded instead of broken, church families don't break up. Broken lives and broken churches come from **UNBROKEN BREAD**.

Endnotes

1. Robert C. Morgan, *Who's Coming To Dinner? Jesus Made Known in the Breaking of Bread*, (Nashville: Abingdon Press, 1992), p. 18.

2. Morgan, p. 18.

3. *The Expositor's Bible Commentary*, Vol.9, "The Acts of The Apostles," (Grand Rapids: Zondervan, 1981), p. 509.

4. W.E. Vine, *An Expository Dictionary of New Testament Words*, (Old Tappan, NJ: Fleming H. Revell, 1940) p. 215.

5. Who knows whether or not the visitor mentioned in 1 Cor. 14:25 was a Christian? The context seems to indicate that he was not.

6. Morgan, p. 19.

7. John W. Ellas, *Clear Choices For Churches*, (Houston: Center for Church Growth, 1994) pp. 12-14.

8. *The Zondervan Pictorial Dictionary*, Merrill C. Tenney, Editor, (Grand Rapids: Zondervan, 1963), p. 808.

9. Vine's, pp. 62-63.

10. Mike Root, *Spilt Grape Juice*, (Joplin, MO: College Press, 1992) p. 14.

11. All of these come from the Sermon on the Mount, Matthew 5-7.

12. Ralph P. Martin, *Worship In The Early Church*, (Grand Rapids: Eerdmans, 1964), p. 10.

13. Robert E. Webber, *Worship Old and New*, (Grand Rapids: Zondervan, 1982), p. 18.

14. James F. White, *Protestant Worship, Traditions in Transition*, (Louisville: Westminster/John Knox Press, 1989), pp. 172-186. See Martin's and Webber's books for additional information.

15. White, pp. 171-186.

16. Vine's, p. 236.

17. Vine's, p. 235.

18. *Webster's New World Dictionary of the American Language*, (Cleveland & New York: The World Publishing Company, 1966), p. 673.

19. Vine's, p. 152.

20. Webster, p. 612.

21. Martin, *Worship In The Early Church*, p. 135.

22. Martin, p. 134.

Bibliography

Ellas, John W. *Clear Choices For Churches*. Houston: Center for Church Growth, 1994.

The Expositor's Bible Commentary, Vol. 9, *The Acts of The Apostles*. Grand Rapids: Zondervan, 1981.

Martin, Ralph P. *Worship In The Early Church*. Grand Rapids: Eerdmans, 1964.

Morgan, Robert C. *Who's Coming To Dinner? Jesus Made Known in the Breaking of Bread*. Nashville: Abingdon Press, 1992.

Root, Mike. *Spilt Grape Juice*. Joplin, MO: College Press, 1992.

Vine, W.E. *An Expository Dictionary of New Testament Words*. Old Tappan, NJ: Fleming H. Revell, 1940.

Webber, Robert E. *Worship Old and New*. Grand Rapids: Zondervan, 1982.

Webster's New World Dictionary of the American Language, Cleveland and New York: The World Publishing Company, 1966.

White, James F. *Protestant Worship, Tradition in Transition*. Louisville: Westminster/John Knox Press, 1989.

The Zondervan Pictorial Dictionary, Merrill C. Tenny, Editor. Grand Rapids: Zondervan, 1963.

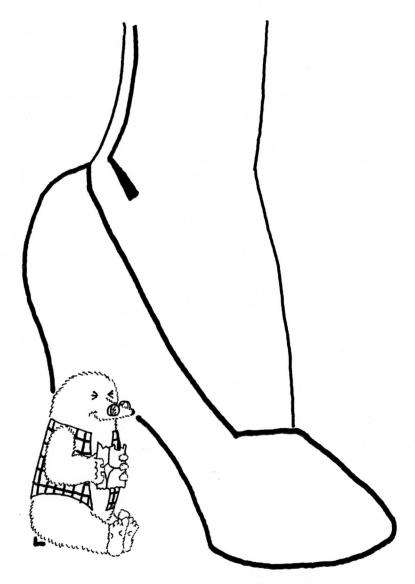

The Shrew in the Pew
By Mike Root
Illustrated by Tim Cox

The smell of furniture polish and lilac perfume assaulted Simon's nose as he peeked through the secret crevice in the floorboard. The hushed tones of whispering and the scraping sound of shuffling feet told him that church was in session at The First Church of Perfect Truth.

No one in the congregation knew about Simon's secret slot. They certainly were unaware of the fact that their church building housed a shrew. They would be deeply disturbed to discover a flaw in their floorboard, but they would be aghast to know they had a shrew in their sanctuary. They knew that a church is people and not a building, but they took great pride in their shiny structure and went to great lengths to keep it clean and free from any type of defilement. That included sin and shrews.

Simon was no ordinary shrew. He was a shrewd shrew. Not many shrews lived to be a senior citizen like Simon. He'd used his head and learned to adjust to life's changes. The Benjamin Franklin glasses resting on the end of his snout allowed him to see things other shrews could only smell. A kelly green plaid vest kept his back and shoulders warm, but did little to cover the expanding paunch that came with old age. In spite of being a recovering cheese-aholic, and a lifetime member of Rodent Watchers, he still was overweight and waddled instead of scurried.

The First Church of Perfect Truth had been Simon's home for most of his life. Most of the time he had the entire place to himself. He lived on the cracker crumbs and Cheerios left behind by small children after the one time they came together each week — Sunday morning from eleven to twelve. Even after old Miss Pickle cleaned up the building on Wednesday afternoon, he found plenty of food in the floor cracks and pew seams.

Usually Simon slept in on Sunday morning to ensure that he was never seen by any of the churchgoers. But this day he decided it was time to live dangerously and do some exploring. There aren't many thrills for old shrews who live in church buildings. So he determined that he was going to see what this strange gathering was all about.

From his snug little hole in the wall, Simon judged the nearest pew to be one and a half football fields away. (Shrews play on small football fields.) He bolted from the security of his apartment and immediately felt naked and exposed. His heart beat fast and his legs worked faster as he sought the safety of under the pew. He was so scared that he forgot about the polished hardwood floors and instead of slowing to a stop he slid to a stop — nose first, right into the pew leg. He almost broke his glasses, but only mashed his muzzle.

Slowly he peeked his beak around the pew leg. What he saw made him gasp. It was a long corridor with giant redwood trees covered in polyester. He saw blue trunks, black trunks, gray trunks, and brown trunks. Each one had a leather planter at the bottom of it. When he saw one huge tree rise up and lay itself across the top of the next one, it dawned on Simon that these were people legs. When a stockinged foot slid from one of the planters, his nose confirmed his suspicions.

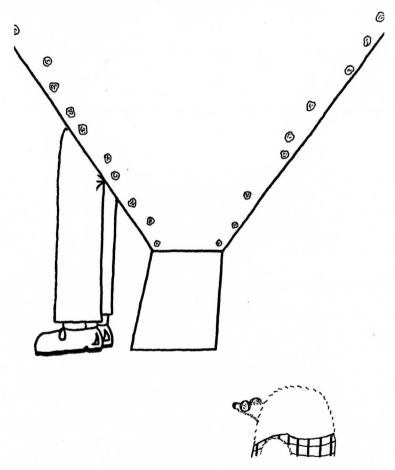

Staying low to the floor he waddled to the next pew. Glancing back at the row of legs he'd just examined, he noticed for the first time that the underside of each pew was covered with warts. At least that's what they looked like. He wiped his glasses with the corner of his vest and looked again. Yes, all along the underside of the pew there were warts, or stalactites, of every shape and color. Pink seemed to be the most popular color, but there were blue, green, and yellow ones, too. He made a note to check on these when all these people left the church building.

The second pew had legs hanging down like the last one, except these were smaller and didn't quite touch the ground. Simon didn't know that he was looking at the legs of Chastity, James and John, but he deduced that they were attached to children. He watched in astonishment as they passed folded pieces of paper to each other under the pew. What was so special about that paper, he wondered. Was that some strange religious ritual for schoolchildren to perform? Simon was now more fascinated than fearful.

Moving to the next pew he found himself next to an enormous imitation leather suitcase. It had slots, zippers and pockets all over, and a long strap that was long enough for it to hang from the owner's shoulders. What could be in there, Simon pondered. The people legs beside it were thin and covered with a see-through material that fit like skin. In fact, it was the same color as skin, but had little holes like a screen.

Mrs Prudence Smythe was completely wrapped up in Preacher Justice's sermon. She whispered, "Amen" and "Praise the Lord," unaware that a shrew was climbing into her purse.

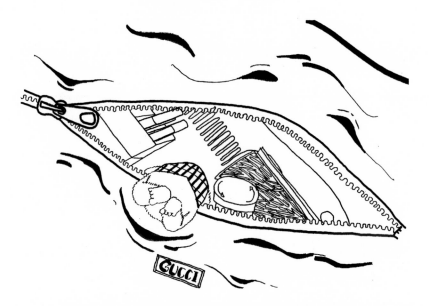

With great trepidation Simon stepped up onto one of the folds in the great suitcase. His heart was pounding so hard that he just knew the skinny-legged giant would hear it. But he was so anxious to see inside the huge bag that he climbed up one of the zippers until he was able to look down into its dark recesses.

What he saw made little sense to him. A package of neatly folded toilet paper? Papers – pins – pencils – little metal cases and long, sweet-smelling tubes of wax. A cardboard box with W-I-N-S-T-O-N printed across the front. An orange bottle with a white cap. It had V-A-L-I-U-M printed on it. What a strange assortment of odd things. He especially thought it was strange that the giant suitcase held a small plastic see-through bag which seemed to hold shredded dried grass. With a "Humph!" of disappointment, Simon slid back to the floor and scurried to the next pew. He scarcely heard Mrs. Smythe's "Praise the Lord."

Turning to inspect the next pew, Simon froze with fear. One of the giants was looking right at him. He was caught. He started to make a mad dash for his baseboard haven when he noticed that the giant wasn't moving to get him. On closer inspection, Simon decided that the giant was sound asleep. He was astonished by the giant's ability to sleep with his head lying on his hand as his elbow rested on a songbook. He chuckled with delight as he imagined what could happen if someone jerked the songbook out from under his elbow.

Sitting next to the sleeping giant was an elderly woman dressed in black. She had a black dress, black screens on her legs, black planters, and a black square box sitting on top of her head. Simon supposed that it was a hat, but with her face buried in a black leather-covered book, the hat looked more like a big bottle top. The big black book had B-I-B-L-E printed on its cover. The elderly woman seemed to be too deeply engrossed in it to notice chubby little Simon as he waddled to the next pew.

Looking back at the woman in black, Simon could now see that she was actually reading another book which was hidden inside the big black book. It was a smaller paperback book. Simon wondered what could be in the book that made the woman blush so much.

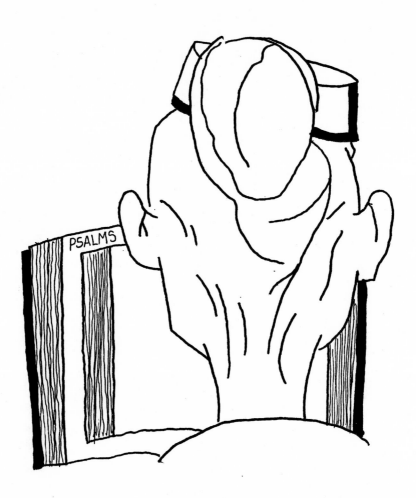

Three sets of legs were the first thing Simon noticed as he turned to inspect the next pew. They were attached to a man who was sitting between two women. They all had their attention directed to the front of the building. The man was holding hands with the woman on his left. Simon thought that was cute. But he couldn't understand why the man was rubbing his foot against the leg of the woman on his right. He decided that humans must not be monogamous in their mating practices. Or, maybe this was a religious practice?

As he continued easing his way toward the back, he was surprised to find the next two pews deserted. There were no legs with planters, or giants of any kind. Only the strange looking warts that seemed to grow under each pew.

Simon was feeling safe as he waddled past the third empty pew. The next pew was the last pew, and as he peeked around to look at it, he was startled to see one lone giant sitting on it.

He was not like the other giants. His skin was brown like acorns, his hair and short whiskers were as silver as icicles. It was obvious to Simon that this man was much poorer than everyone else he'd seen in the First Church of Perfect Truth. His clothes were old, worn and dirty. But unlike everyone else, he had a sparkle in his eye and laugh wrinkles on either side of his mouth. In his right hand he was clutching a small, well-used, black, leather-bound book just like the one the elderly woman had.

When Simon's eyes finished examining the elderly man from head to toe, he had an eerie feeling that he was being watched. As he looked up he jumped when he realized that the man was looking right at him. Simon's heart pounded like a grandfather clock and his legs refused to work. Then he realized that the man was smiling at him. His eyes were bright and kind, and his smile reminded Simon of the rainbow he'd seen through the church window one day. Simon calmed down so quickly and was so relaxed that it hardly surprised him when the giant whispered, "Hi there, little fellow."

He said it as if talking to shrews was commonplace for him.

"Don't be afraid," he said, "I love all of God's little

creatures. What are you doing here? I've never seen a shrew in church before."

Simon looked around, as if someone might be eavesdropping, and squeaked, "I'm exploring. I've never been out here when the giants were here, and I wanted to see what was going on. Oh — my name is Simon."

"Well, Simon, my name is Gabe. That's short for Gabriel." Reaching down with his huge hand open and his palm up, he said, "Hop on board and come up here beside me."

Before Simon even thought it through he was in the man's hand and soon sitting in the pew next to him. There was something about the old dark-skinned man that made Simon want to trust him completely.

The man then reached into his coat pocket and brought out a few cracker crumbs for Simon. Simon ate them gratefully, as his stomach was starting to growl. All the while the man continued talking to Simon in a voice so soothing that Simon felt totally at ease.

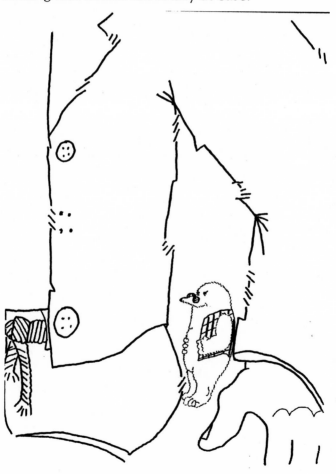

Simon was very impressed with the man's friendliness. He had never dreamed that one of the giants would be so kind. Without thinking, Simon blurted out, "Why is no one sitting with you?"

The man's face clouded in thought, then it broke into a big smile as he declared, "I suppose these folks don't know how special I am."

"Special?" asked Simon as he looked over the man's tattered clothing.

"Sure," he said with a muffled laugh. I give them a chance to help someone who is poor. They didn't have to go lookin' 'cause I jus' came to 'em. They could help me with clothes, or food or even a place to stay. You see, I am an opportunity for them."

As Simon saw how far away everyone sat from Gabe and how much finer their clothes were, his mind became troubled by some questions.

"How long have you been coming here?" he asked.

"Oh — 'bout two months now," he replied softly.

"And how many of these people have helped you in the last two months?"

Gabe cleared his throat and thought a moment. "Well, old sister Pearl gave me some food once after everyone had left. She didn't want anyone to see her doing it."

Simon straightened up and urged him on with, "And?"

The sparkle disappeared from Gabe's eyes and he stared at the floor. "Well," he said finally, "no one else has ever acted like I existed. They kind of look right through me."

"Why?" cried Simon. He couldn't imagine anyone not wanting to help this kind man.

With sad countenance Gabe continued, "Simon, there's a lot you don't know about humans. You see, I'm a different color than the rest of these folks. My clothes are in rags while they have fine, church-going apparel. They live in fine houses and I, well, I just sleep wherever it's warm.

"I guess," he said as he scratched his head, "because I'm so different from them, they're a little afraid of me."

His head and his shoulders slumped.

Simon was heartbroken. A small tear rolled down his muzzle and came to rest on his spectacles.

"Gabe," he said with a crack in his voice, "If these folks never give you clothes, never give you food, and are never kind to you, why do you keep coming back here week after week?"

Like a Morning Glory stroked by the sun's rays, Gabe slowly straightened his back, raised his head, and a big smile blossomed on his face. Simon must have said the magic word.

Gabe's eyes sparkled again as he whispered, "Simon, I'm gonna tell ya a secret. Can you keep a secret?"

Simon, still in shock from the sudden change in Gabe, slowly nodded his head in the affirmative.

"Let me read you something from the Good Book, Simon. This is God's message to mankind."

He deftly flipped the pages of his old, worn book until he found the place he was looking for. Simon leaned his little head forward to hear every word.

"It says here in the Good Book, in Hebrews, Chapter 13, verse 2, 'Do not neglect to show hospitality to strangers, for by this some have entertained angels without knowing it.'" Then he gently closed the book.

Simon looked down at the pew as he contemplated what Gabe had read. His mind worked it over like a baker kneading dough. Strangers. Hospitality. Entertain angels. Without knowing it. Bingo!

Simon quickly looked up at Gabe, who grinned like he was about to burst. Then with that familiar sparkle in his eye, he gave Simon a big wink.

Simon thought, "Gabe, Gabriel. Where have I heard that name before?"

About the Author

Mike Root graduated from Harding University, earned an M.A. in History from George Mason University, and a Master of Theology from Trinity Theological Seminary. After a two-year ministry with a church in Benton, Arkansas, he became the pulpit minister with the Fairfax Church of Christ in Fairfax, Virginia. During his thirteen-year ministry there, the congregation grew from 175 to over 800. For eight years of that ministry Mike served as a volunteer Police Chaplain for the Fairfax County Police Department. In July of 1990, he accepted the position of pulpit minister for the Altamesa church in Ft. Worth, Texas.

Mike has also authored *Rev* (a novel about life as a Police Chaplain), published by University Editions; as well as two previous books with College Press: *Spilt Grape Juice: Rethinking the Worship Tradition* and *Life's Cobwebs*.

Mike and his wife, Donna, have three children: Deborah, Elizabeth, and Jonathan.

THE SHREW IN THE PEW